Pedagogies for Diverse Learners

Pedagogies for Diverse Learners

Tools for Discovery and Development

Edited by

Sarah J. Noonan

ROWMAN & LITTLEFIELD
Lanham • Boulder • New York • London

Published by Rowman & Littlefield
An imprint of The Rowman & Littlefield Publishing Group, Inc.
4501 Forbes Boulevard, Suite 200, Lanham, Maryland 20706
www.rowman.com

86-90 Paul Street, London EC2A 4NE

Copyright © 2023 by Sarah J. Noonan

All rights reserved. No part of this book may be reproduced in any form or by any electronic or mechanical means, including information storage and retrieval systems, without written permission from the publisher, except by a reviewer who may quote passages in a review.

British Library Cataloguing in Publication Information Available

Library of Congress Cataloging-in-Publication Data

Names: Noonan, Sarah J., 1949- editor.
Title: Pedagogies for diverse learners : tools for discovery and development / edited by Sarah J. Noonan.
Description: Lanham : Rowman & Littlefield, [2023] | Includes bibliographical references.
Identifiers: LCCN 2023023976 (print) | LCCN 2023023977 (ebook) | ISBN 9781475855937 (cloth) | ISBN 9781475855944 (paperback) | ISBN 9781475855951 (ebook)
Subjects: LCSH: Effective teaching. | Inclusive education.
Classification: LCC LB1025.3 .P43425 2023 (print) | LCC LB1025.3 (ebook) | DDC 371.102--dc23/eng/20230626
LC record available at https://lccn.loc.gov/2023023976
LC ebook record available at https://lccn.loc.gov/2023023977

Contents

Preface   vii
    Sarah Noonan

Acknowledgments   xi

Chapter 1: Reclaiming Our Native Youth   1
    Penelope Dupris

Chapter 2: Radical Listening and Love: Introduction to Social Justice and Healing Pedagogies   21
    Aura Wharton-Beck

Chapter 3: Designing Learning Activities Using Social Justice and Healing Pedagogies   33
    Aura Wharton-Beck

Chapter 4: The Changing Nature of Stress for Adult Learners in a Post-Pandemic World   49
    Derrick Crim

Chapter 5: The Secret Sauce of Exemplary Educators   71
    Gail L. Weinhold

Chapter 6: My American Story: Storytelling and Songwriting Projects for Social Change   87
    Ilah Raleigh

Chapter 7: The Centrality of Identity in the Learning Environment   109
    Jayne Sommers and Christina Holmgren

Chapter 8: Academic Student Procrastination: Causes and Effects on Student Learning   129
    Sarah Noonan

Chapter 9: Prevention, Intervention, and Recovery Pedagogies to
    Disrupt Academic Underachievement and Procrastination   149
    Sarah Noonan

Chapter 10: Dear Professor: Inventing New Pedagogies   173
    Sarah Noonan

Index   177

About the Contributors   183

Preface

Sarah Noonan

Pedagogies for Diverse Learners: Tools for Discovery and Development offers profiles of diverse learners as well as the specific learning and teaching strategies needed to foster students' sense of belonging and well-being, visibility, experiences of deep learning, academic achievement, and personal transformation. Instead of exploring the "what" and "how" of learning and teaching first, the focus is on the "who," namely the diverse students enrolled in your class. The recommended strategies make sense based on student characteristics and needs and academic achievement goals.

Strategies to recognize and value diverse student identities, experiences, and preferred ways of learning appear throughout the book. *Tools for Discovery and Development* facilitates continued growth in knowledge, skills, and dispositions as well as the practical applications of learning to "real life." The *discovery phase* involves participation in formal and informal episodes of learning, gaining knowledge, and assessing the new learnings' potential value and uses. The *development phase* occurs when subsequent small or large changes in thinking and acting occur, and potentially result in the experience of "incremental or transformational learning" (Mezirow, 2000).

Pedagogies for Diverse Learners addresses the cognitive, affective, and behavioral aspects of learning and teaching. An underlying assumption held about all students involves the belief that students do not arrive as a blank slate. Their family, cultural, and educational circumstances and experiences accompany them as they enter the physical or virtual space for learning. Appreciating students' background and experiences goes a long way toward forming relationships with students.

Differentiated strategies based on learner characteristics and needs also include ethical teaching and learning practices, such as the right to be seen and appreciated, the experience of nurturing relationships between teachers, students, and peers, a positive learning environment, and *the expectation as well as the experience of academic success*.

Opportunities to differentiate the curriculum based on learner characteristics and needs include the modification of the "content, process, products, and [affect] learning environment" (Maker, 1982; Tomlison, 2014). The modifications offer different pathways to achieve learning goals. The "affect" involves positive relationships and the *emotional support* found in inviting, growth-oriented, and accessible learning environments, which affect students' perception of schooling and educational systems.

To meet the needs of diverse learners, social justice leadership and anti-oppressive practices in education are needed. A study of principals found social justice leaders and leadership involved the following five actions: "demonstrate social justice, challenge the status quo, exercise critical instructional leadership, shape and preserve respectful relationships, and honour [sic] voice" (Kowalchuk, 2019, para. 8). All five practices begin with "action" verbs and may involve significant changes in perspectives, learning and teaching strategies, greater emphasis on teacher-student relationships, and hearing and honoring student voice using radical listening.

Anti-oppressive practice expands the idea of who is a diverse learner. As defined by Aquil et al. (2021), "anti-oppressive practice recognizes the oppression that exists in our society/space and aims to mitigate the effects of oppression and eventually equalize the power imbalances that exist between people" (para. 3). Anti-oppressive practice recognizes that "all forms of oppression are interconnected in some way, shape or form" (para. 3). The definition of anti-oppressive practice involves the knowledge of oppression and its effects, as well as a clear focus: *mitigate* the effects of oppression and *equalize* power imbalances.

Ignoring and undervaluing family histories and cultures may cause students to disengage and lose interest in learning. Useful ways to engage students in interpreting their experiences involve raising "critical consciousness, [participating in] equitable and mindful learning environments, acknowledging context, and [providing] student opportunities to learn using anti-oppressive techniques" (Aquil et al., 2021, para. 37). For example, teaching students about the language of inequality, like the meaning of the terms, "power 'and' privilege," should occur long before students enter higher education, and deepen as more is known.

Using the larger definition of diverse learners found in anti-oppressive practice, ten key *Pedagogies for Diverse Learners: Tools for Discovery and Development* are featured throughout this book. The pedagogies address the study of the history and present-day experiences of diverse learners and communities, the elements needed to maximize student engagement in learning, and students' experiences of nurturing and trustworthy relationships and the support needed to ensure academic success. The pedagogies for diverse learners offer students opportunities to

1. investigate the past and current practice of oppression and its effects, use of privilege and power to maintain the status quo; and the experience of intergenerational trauma.
2. engage in radical listening, critical reflection, and dialogue for learning and transformation.
3. use critical consciousness and the language of inequality to critique and challenge dominant assumptions and practices.
4. experience nurturing relationships, whole-person health, and inclusive learning environments.
5. engage in authentic, interdisciplinary, collaborative learning projects and assessments, participate in social learning, and use problem-solving methods.
6. experience joyful learning, which benefits students now and later in their lives.
7. experience how student identities, learning styles, perspectives, and experiences are recognized and honored.
8. identify the root causes of academic disengagement and learn the strategies, habits, and dispositions needed to raise academic performance.
9. receive an invitation to learn and experience hope, and benefit from goals, structure, coaching, and "fast" feedback needed to disrupt a pattern of academic underachievement and procrastination.
10. experience empathy and compassion, and trust their teachers' commitment to see them through the learning process.

Descriptions and examples of the above pedagogies can be found in many of the chapters along with more specific pedagogies, such as affective and social justice and healing pedagogies.

Meeting the needs of diverse learners enriches the educational experiences of *all* students. When teachers and professors learn with their students, they experience change, and transformation becomes possible for both students and their teachers. The process of learning begins with a focus on students.

REFERENCES

Aquil, A. R., Malik, M., Jacques, K. A., Lee, K., Parker, L. J., Kennedy, C. E., Mooney, G., & German, D. (2021). Engaging in anti-oppressive public health teaching: Challenges and recommendations. *Pedagogy in Health Promotion*, 7(4), 344–353. https://doi.org/10.1177/23733799211045407

Kowalchuk, D. (2019). Voices for change: Social justice leadership practices. *Journal of Educational Leadership and Policy Studies, Special Issue #1 on Educational Leadership and Social Justice*, 3(1).

Maker, C. J. (1982). *Curriculum development for the gifted and talented*. Aspect Systems.

Mezirow, J. (2000). *Learning as transformation: Critical perspectives on a theory in progress* (1st ed.). Jossey-Bass.

Tomlison, C. (2014). *How to differentiate curriculum in mixed-ability classrooms* (2nd ed.). Association for Supervision and Curriculum Development (ASCD).

Acknowledgments

I feel so grateful to be in the good company of students and colleagues for all the years of my life and career. Students taught me quite a few lessons about learning and teaching, often without saying a word. I truly enjoyed knowing all the students and look forward to meeting new students. During every interaction and learning experience, there is a chance to cross a threshold and enter a new room with so much more to learn.

I appreciate and admire the knowledge, scholarship, and wisdom of my colleagues who contributed to this book. Many thanks go to contributors Derrick Crim, Penny Dupris, Christine Holmgren, Ilah Raleigh, Jayne Sommers, Gail Weinhold, and Aura Wharton-Beck. Thanks go to Dr. Candace Chou for serving and sometimes saving us in her role as the chair of the Educational Leadership Department at the University of St. Thomas.

The chapters describe something that is hard to find, namely the learning and teaching strategies that attract diverse learners to engage in learning, particularly in a "post" pandemic world. Thank you for your friendship and contributions to this book. I truly enjoyed working and writing with you. You provided solid advice on effective and engaging learning for all students.

My thanks go to my daughter Jessica Noonan for her creativity in the design of the figures in the book. I thank Carlie Wall, Tom Koerner, Tricia Currie-Knight, and Jasmine Holman of Rowman and Littlefield for their patience and encouraging feedback. I appreciate the gift of the reviewers' time and effort needed to read, evaluate, and endorse *Pedagogies for Diverse Learners*. Many thanks go to Kathlene Holmes Campbell, PhD, Latanya Daniels, EdD, Duchess Harris, JD and PhD, and Jason Wenschlag, EdD.

This page acknowledges the contributions of all those involved in this project with an open invitation: The door is always open at Park Avenue, and there is a place at the desk or table for you. Many thanks go to my friends and family for your continued love and support—you mean the world to me.

Chapter 1

Reclaiming Our Native Youth

Penelope Dupris

Colleges and universities across multiple states now offer waived tuition for Native American students. The aim of waiving tuition for Native students reflects a recent concerted effort to increase post-secondary enrollment and an attempt to make reparations for the historical mistreatment of Native scholars in the U.S. schools (Hall, 2022). Ultimately, these increased endeavors promoting Native student enrollment will transform the diversity in post-secondary campuses. Native students' enrollment in post-secondary education will likely increase.

This chapter begins with Native students' experiences in a predominantly White K–12 education system. These experiences impact Native students' entry, participation, and success in college. The story of Native history and experience of trauma is largely an absent narrative in predominantly White schools and communities. The Native story told in this chapter is tied to the land—a sacred place that holds the lives, proud traditions, and culture of one Tribal nation.

The point of telling this research story about how Native students' experience of "school" from the perspective of Native students, parents, and community members is to uncover how Native student experiences inside the school and in the community affect Native student participation and success in school.

The Native students who experience racism in their high school will soon enter a college classroom, taking their high school experience of "school" with them. This chapter provides an insider's view of Native values and culture as well as the perspectives of Native families, school liaisons, administrators, parents, and teachers about the public school system.

The central themes of the Native student experience described in this chapter include (1) intergenerational effects from historical trauma; (2) Native students' experiences of implicit bias and racism in schools; and (3) the need for a personal connection within the school's curriculum and culture. The chapter concludes with a description of Native pedagogies, including the strategies needed to implement a culturally relevant curriculum.

The true story about Native student experiences begins with a description of the two worlds experienced by students from the "Eagle River Indian Community" (a pseudonym used to ensure confidentiality). The findings from my case study of Native students' experiences in high school demonstrated that not enough people know much about Native experiences. After reading about the school system from Native families and students, the Native pedagogies make sense based on the "who" is learning as well as "why" certain learning and teaching activities invite students to learn and grow as a preparation for college. The story begins with Native students living in two worlds.

THE DICHOTOMY OF TWO SCHOOL COMMUNITIES

Like most midwestern Tribal reservations and communities, entering Tribal lands would be indiscernible if it were not for the signs. At first glance, midwestern Tribal reservations tend to depict their neighboring towns. The architecture of the homes, businesses, and buildings mirror the architecture of most midwestern communities.

Some midwestern Tribal reservations and communities have a billboard-sized sign welcoming people to their Tribal nation as they enter. Approaching Eagle River Indian Community is an event. Billboards advertising the casino and promoting recent high-dollar payouts remind tourists of the purpose for their visit. When crossing over and entering Tribal land, it is easy to miss the Tribal community welcome sign. The casino and hotel sign commands attention and beckons adventurers to come and play.

Eagle River Indian Community has the standard baseball field and convenience store that most small midwestern towns offer. The small, hometown feeling echoes surrounding communities. The fact that this town is on designated Tribal land might be forgettable, if not for the constant reminders posted throughout the community. Building signs, including the water tower, proudly display the Tribal name or Tribal flag. Even the residential road signs bear Native names. All these signs serve as constant reminders that non-Natives are guests on Tribal land. As a guest, you have no incentive to stay beyond the casino trip.

For Natives, however, the Tribal signs represent home, a place of refuge. Tribal nation and Tribal flags represent Native pride. The signs speak to the Tribe's resilience. The signs also serve as a teaching point to Native youth and as a constant reminder to Tribal members that they are, in fact, sovereign.

The U.S. government imposed genocidal efforts to extinguish their Tribal ancestors, including forced relocation, war and imprisonment, stolen lands, broken treaties, poverty, and starvation throughout history (Spring, 1997; Takaki, 2008). This Tribe found the funds to buy back their stolen land and eventually flourish, even though the U.S. government proceeded to flood livable Tribal land and burial mounds. Tribal flags posted throughout the community are indeed significant because the signs proudly represent survival, strength, ancestry, cultural values, and an inextinguishable resistance to colonization.

Living in Eagle River Indian Community is comparable to other midwestern Tribal reservations. It is not a place without devastating consequences. Historical trauma has placed a heavy toll throughout Indian Country (Brave Heart, 2000; Brave Heart & DeBruyn, 1998; Brown-Rice, 2013; Evans-Campbell, 2008). Tribal nations throughout the U.S. are lovingly referred to as "Indian Country" among Native Americans. Some families in the Tribal community thrive, while other families have their own personal challenges resulting from historical trauma.

Stories about substance abuse, teen suicide, poverty, and defeatism provide the narrative for what plagues Indian Country. Poverty and trauma serve as a common and an unfortunate communal experience. Eagle River is not exempt from the impacts of historical trauma. However, tragedy is like storm clouds covering the sun. When the storm clouds part, the sun shines brightly. The beauty and reverence in the Tribal community can be fully seen and appreciated, despite its areas of hardship.

Eagle River Indian community has not only survived but thrived. Cultural norms and teachings have preserved their identity. Despite all odds and historical oppression, Tribal members have shown an incredible amount of resilience and have been able to retain their rights to Tribal sovereignty.

Eagle River Indian Community differs from other Tribal reservations across the U.S. because Eagle River does not have its own Tribal school. Native youth are bussed to a neighboring school district that serves a predominantly White population. Education is a highly regarded cultural component to the Tribe. As a result, Native youth are asked to succeed in a White educational institution. Native youth leave the safety and refuge of their Tribal community and are asked to adhere to and compete within White cultural norms.

Leaving the reservation for the neighboring White suburban town is momentous. The bus commute takes less than ten minutes but leaves a lasting impression on Native students. Siblings and neighbors from kindergarten through high school are crammed three to a seat. The bus leaves the reservation, situated within a river valley, and climbs up the curving, canyon roads to the adjacent town. The students' ears pop as they make the ascent to the school that may not honor their Native cultural norms. This serves as a physical sign that they are about to become an outsider. Native student safety nets are no longer securely in place.

High schoolers watch their younger siblings depart at the elementary and middle school. Siblings are now separated and will not reunite until the end of the school day. Older siblings have no control of what lies ahead for their younger siblings. They can no longer protect and provide them with a sense of comfort and security. This feeling is reminiscent of boarding schools. Young Native children were forcibly removed from their homes to attend state-run boarding schools or religious affiliated boarding schools.

Although Native youth in the Eagle River Indian community attend public school and did not experience the trauma of boarding schools, some of their parents and grandparents certainly did. Native families are consoled knowing that reunification occurs daily after the school day. The last school bell finally rings, an auditory sign Native siblings will once again reunite.

The trek is made back to the reservation on the yellow school bus. Once again, Native students' ears pop as they descend into their Tribal community. This physical sign is a representation that they are almost home. Students are back within the confines of their community, back to their place of refuge.

In contrast, Native students attend school in East River Bend, a quiet, Midwestern town of approximately 16,000 people. Situated along a major river, East River Bend offers breathtaking views of surrounding bluffs, lush greenery, and majestic eagles soaring in the sky. Driving into the town itself presents quite a scenic view. Nestled between pristine farms, it is common to see horses grazing among picket fences and towering rock formations. The scenic highway dips down and curves to the left and right as it approaches the town. Directional signs advertise biking trails, canoeing, tubing, and kayaking along the river.

Like most towns along the river, the landscape of East River Bend is terraced. Smaller, older homes line the streets surrounding the historic downtown. Further up the hill, away from the river, mid-size, middle-class homes create a residential feel to the town. Playgrounds, parks, and hiking trails are sprinkled in between these homes. Multimillion-dollar homes, with walls of windows, sit on top of the hill overlooking the river. Although the town feels economically diverse, the population is mainly White.

East River Bend provides a small-town lifestyle to residents. Like typical small towns, people in East River Bend know each other, their families, and even their business. Relationships and connections are valued in East River Bend, including the generation of graduates who now enroll their children in the same school.

Although small in stature, East River Bend supports an active art community. East River Bend's rugged beauty and proximity to the river appeals to the town's residents. Although East River Bend seems like the ideal small town, Native American students experience the town differently.

Approximately 80 Native American students from a neighboring reservation attend the East River Bend school district and comprise 3% of the school district's population. Native students navigate the school and town with effort in contrast to their White peers.

Some residents in East River Bend do not see the overt acts of racism in the community. Instead, Hanson, a school administrator, believed their town engaged in "some underlying issues of racism . . . and closed-mindedness, however, the racism appears to be more hidden."

Native students adapted to the White community by knowing the expected norms and hiding some of their Tribal culture until the students returned home. Administrators know Native youth, who traverse between the adjacent community and the reservation walk in two worlds. Students engage in code-switching to fit in, even in uncomfortable places. Code-switching is a term explaining how students of color demonstrate White cultural norms to fit in a White dominant school or community. Native students experience challenges unlike their White peers in East River Bend because of historical trauma and dominant White culture.

THE INTERGENERATIONAL EFFECTS FROM HISTORICAL TRAUMA

Understanding historical trauma and recognizing the intergenerational effects is paramount to Native student success. Historical trauma for Indigenous people began with colonization and relocation efforts. Trauma passed down through multiple generations is defined as intergenerational trauma. The Native experience of boarding schools is named as the precursor for intergenerational trauma.

Native American boarding schools began in the 1860s and continued to operate until the late 1970s (Mejia, n.d.; Pember, 2019). Boarding schools were designed to assimilate Native children into mainstream society and eradicate their Native culture. Historically, Native youth were taken from their homes and bussed hundreds of miles away to attend boarding schools (Reyhner & Eder, 2004). Native parents living in poverty could not access their children. Families were separated for the entire school year. Reunification often led to heartbreak as Native children were stripped of their cultural identity and assimilated to White cultural norms.

Boarding schools operated in a paramilitary structure requiring students to wear uniforms, perform manual labor for half the day, and receive instruction the remainder of the day (Reyhner & Eder, 2004; Spring, 1997). In the

1920s a variety of investigations were published indicating the deplorable conditions and abuse Native children faced while attending boarding school (Spring, 1997). The Meriam Report highlighted how underfunded boarding schools led to student death from malnutrition, tuberculosis, and trachoma (Reyhner & Eder, 2004).

A loss of language prevented communication between Native grandchildren and their grandparents (Spring, 1997). Many Native students in boarding schools experienced physical abuse, sexual abuse, malnourishment, and chronic disease. Some Native students died while attending boarding schools. Their bodies, buried in unmarked graves, were never returned to their families.

Subsequently, Native families resented governmental authority and the forcible educational practices imposed upon their children (Reyhner & Eder, 2004). Educational institutions could not be trusted as they served as a weapon for colonization. The impacts of government-sanctioned boarding schools among Native families are felt today.

Boarding schools were named as the precursor of intergenerational trauma. Tribal members and administrators from a case study of Native students and families identified broken homes, mental health issues, substance abuse, and violence as some of the intergenerational impacts of trauma. Trauma created a chain reaction that occurred throughout multiple generations. Mental health issues led to substance abuse. Substance abuse and violence separated families. Children were removed from homes and families, including the families who were previously victimized by boarding schools.

Multiple studies and peer-reviewed articles describe the intergenerational effects within the Native community from boarding schools. Educators were either unaware boarding schools existed or did not fully realize how boarding schools continued to impact Native families.

Boarding schools still existed until 1974, meaning students may know how their parents or grandparents may have been victimized by those schools. The boarding school reality is not a history of 150 years ago—it's a reality within our lifetimes. The boarding school experience continued to impact Native families. Schools never rectified the racialized harm. Native students often felt mistreated while attending school. As a result, a lot of Native students dropped out of school. These former Native students are now grandparents and parents to the current Native students in East River Bend.

The cultural mistrust between Native families and schools has been passed down to multiple generations. Consequently, Native parents show resistance about engaging with teachers and administrators. Educators failed to recognize how intergenerational trauma affected Native parent engagement in schools. Instead, Native parents and their parenting styles were blamed. Kingbird, a school liaison, described the effects of the educational system:

> Public school systems . . . [are] not a good place for our kids and our families. Grandma didn't graduate. Mom didn't graduate . . . Parents were treated, I'm going to say poorly, and that's an understatement, in the school.

Elders living in the Tribal communities may have been impacted by boarding schools, resulting in negative attitudes about public education. The United States released a report from the Interior Department that shed light on the historical trauma resulting from boarding schools in May 2022. Fifty-three burial sites were identified across schools (Brooks, 2022). Deb Haaland, the interior secretary, said in response to the report,

> The federal policies that attempted to wipe out Native identity, language, and culture continue to manifest in the pain Tribal communities face today, including cycles of violence and abuse, disappearance of Indigenous people, premature deaths, poverty and loss of wealth, mental health disorders, and substance abuse. Recognizing the impacts of the federal Indian boarding school system cannot just be a historical reckoning. We must also chart a path forward to deal with these legacy issues. (Brooks, 2022, para. 1)

Perhaps the United States is learning from Canada's mistake. In 2008, the prime minister of Canada made an unprecedented move by publicly apologizing for the intergenerational consequences of boarding schools as part of its Truth and Reconciliation Commission. In 2015, the finalized investigation was completed and released. Since the release of the investigation, Canada has taken little action toward reconciliation. Pope Francis visited Canada in July 2022 and publicly apologized:

> I ask forgiveness, in particular, for the ways in which many members of the Church and of religious communities cooperated, not least through their indifference, in projects of cultural destruction and forced assimilation promoted by the governments of that time, which culminated in the system of residential schools. (Humayun, Isaac, & Newton, 2022, para. 27)

While some Natives felt validated, other Natives expressed the uselessness of apologies. Henry Boubard, an 80-year-old residential school survivor said, "You took away my education, you took away my life, you took away my marriage, you took away my identity, you took away everything I wanted to be. Now it's nothing, and you say I'm sorry" (Humayun, Isaac, & Newton, 2022, para. 32). Chief Desmond Bull suggested,

> If you want to help us heal, stop telling us to get over it. . . . We can't get over it when intergenerational trauma impacts every youth and every member, every family who had a residential school survivor. Instead of getting over it, I'm

asking you to get with it, get with learning about our history, get with learning about our culture, our people, who we are. (Associated Press, 2022, para. 6)

School administrators and Tribal members pleaded for increased support. The repetitive cycle of intergenerational trauma affects Native students. School liaisons report concerns over student well-being and mental health. More students struggle and the level of mental health concerns worry educators.

Kingbird, a director sponsored by the Tribe, summed this up by saying, "And we know . . . those families. Because those challenges are again mending that sacred hoop. Their sacred hoop isn't mended yet." The sacred hoop is another term for the medicine wheel. It is used as a metaphor for breaking and healing the generational and systemic cycle of generational poverty, abuse, and trauma.

NATIVE STUDENTS' EXPERIENCES INVOLVING RACISM AND IMPLICIT BIAS IN SCHOOL

In 2015, the East River Bend boys' basketball team played against another high school team. The East River Bend's most valuable player was Native. The opposing team defeated East River Bend and two players boasted racial remarks about the Native student over social media. One student tweeted, "It was the Squaw Creek Massacre at . . . [the] gymnasium tonight" (RE Sports, 2015, para. 5). Another student tweeted, "[Student's Name] recreated the trail of tears tonight" (Boese, 2015, February 19, para. 4).

Local news reported that the two students involved received disciplinary action according to school policy and the state's high school league bylaws (Hyatt, 2015; RE Sports, 2015). However, coaches from both teams gave differing perspectives on the matter. The East River Bend's assistant coach, and father of this Native student, said,

> I don't think everybody realizes or understands the story behind the Trail of Tears, or what the definition of "squaw" means. It's horrible. The first thing that came to my mind when "squaw" was mentioned was my mother (and) my grandmother who raised my older brother and myself. My grandmother is full-blooded, born in the early 1900s, she dealt with a lot of these issues. It hit home. (RE Sports, 2015, para. 11)

In contrast, the opposing team's coach was more casual. They stated, "It's just moving on. It's a situation where hopefully for future years, it hits home with the guys we have and we can reference down the road. It's just one [instance,] we have to move on from right now" (Boese, 2015, February 19, para. 7).

Although the school district has not made national news since 2015, Native students continued to experience racism. Peterson, a school administrator, compared racial slurs experienced by Native students to African American students: "I would dare say that we probably had more incidents with a White student using a racial slur with the Native students than we did with a White student using a racial slur with an African American student." A Native student had their long hair pulled and was called a "prairie N-word" by a White student. In another incident a White student told the Native student, "Scalp me, daddy." See figure 1.1.

Native students with lighter skin or who may not vocally represent their identity as Native, navigated school easier. Light-skinned Native students may experience "White passing," and do not necessarily experience the same level of racism as their peers.

School communities are meant to provide a safe space for students to learn and thrive. Yet, many Native students report personal experiences of implicit bias from classmates and teachers. While racist acts are blatant and obvious, implicit bias is subdued. The Perception Institute (n.d.) defined implicit bias as "a preference (or aversion to) a person or group of people. . . . [Implicit bias] describe[s] when we have attitudes towards people or associate stereotypes with them without our conscious knowledge" (para. 1).

A common example of implicit bias included the assumption that all Native students were cultural experts. Teachers called on Native students by asking questions: "How do you say this in Dakota?" or, "What do you know about

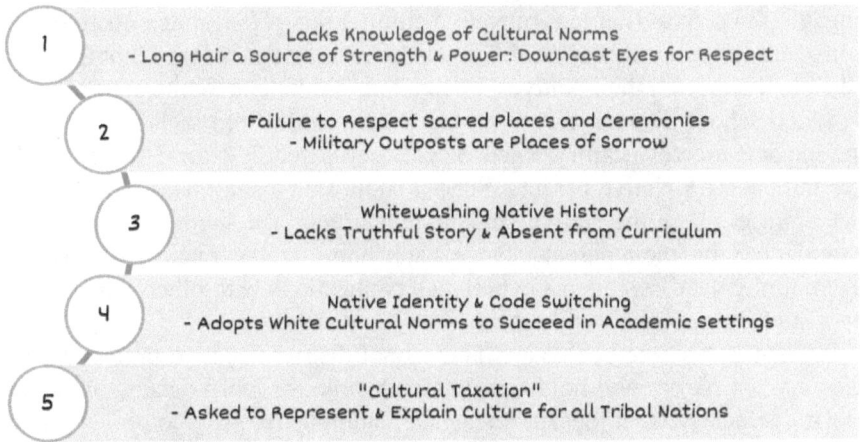

Figure 1.1. Native Students' Experiences of Racism and Implicit Bias.
Source: Created by Jessica Jo Noonan.

this topic?" The concept of "cultural taxation" refers to the expectation that an individual is asked to speak for a culture and use their racial or ethnic identity to stand in for all Tribal members (Padilla, 1994, p. 26).

Padilla (1994) explained the "cultural obligations" of a diverse ethnic identity regarding the obligation to serve on committees and/or respond to a crisis after receiving a call from the administration. This service does not support "academic excellence" and tenure decisions, and drains faculty of time and energy.

Native students feel uncomfortable in class. In another incident, a teacher refused to honor sacredness within Native culture. This incident involved a social studies teacher presenting a lesson on Sundance.

When a Native student asked their teacher to stop, the teacher dismissed the student's request. Thomas, a school mentor for Native students recalled,

> One of my students, an 8th grader, said "You can't show this." And the teacher said, "Why?" And he said, "Because it's a ceremony. It's sacred to us." And she started arguing with the student [in] the middle of class. He cried and he left.

Additionally, Native students do not feel welcomed or liked by their teachers. Prejudice created hardship for some Native students. Some Native students had a hard time remaining in class, feeling their teachers did not care about them. Cultural misunderstandings prevented positive relationships between educators and students. Using downcast eyes, and not directly responding to the speaker is part of this communication problem.

Some educators perceived Native students as defiant or disrespectful when they avoided eye contact. White cultural norms differ from Native cultural norms. Most Tribal nations teach their youth to avoid eye contact while engaging in active listening. In Native culture, this physical demonstration is considered respectful. For Native students in East River Bend, some White educators expected their Native students to assimilate to White culture.

When school districts fail to protect Native kids from racialized trauma, the impacts are devastating. Racist acts experienced by Native students trigger trauma with Native parents. School should be a safe place for learning, not a place where the Native students experience the same type of trauma experienced by their parents. Once back home at the Eagle River Indian Community, Native students experience connections with other Tribal members, and feel the safety of home.

Racism is a learned behavior. The school district needs to protect Native kids against racism and hold people responsible for racist acts. Quite a few racist incidents occur because teachers, administrators, and/or classroom aides failed to understand Native history and culture. Racism adversely affects students' decisions to engage in learning.

THE NEED FOR A PERSONAL CONNECTION WITHIN THE SCHOOL'S CURRICULUM AND CULTURE

Navigating a systemically White school district proved challenging for Native students. Native students in East River Bend were often expected to code-switch. Code-switching is a term explaining how students of color demonstrate White cultural norms to fit in. Code-switching placed an emotional toll on Native students and increased a sense of identity loss.

Native students were tasked with pushing aside their own cultural identities and sense of self to succeed in academic settings. An absentee narrative solidified a disconnect and loss of identity for Native students in school. Most teachers in East River Bend identified as White and taught content areas from a patriarchal, White cultural lens. Native culture, literature, history, and social issues were not explicitly taught or embedded in all content areas.

Absentee narratives contributed to an identity crisis for Native youth. An absentee narrative exists in schools when the histories, cultures, and personal narratives of people of color are subconsciously or deliberately excluded from the curriculum. Students of color lose the opportunity to see themselves and their culture represented within a prescribed White curriculum.

For example, a Tribal member explains the importance of long hair: "A lot of our kids [including] the boys have braids." Many Native boys braided their long hair. However, a Native boy with long braided hair in a classroom full of White students creates an anomaly. White students are not accustomed to this Native cultural norm. An underrepresentation of Native identities and culture exists in classroom communities. As a result, Native boys are often teased for their long hair.

Native youth surpass standards when performing on the powwow trail and could exhibit the same behavior in class when educators gave them an opportunity to do so. A Tribal leader explains how the absentee narrative prevented Native students from thriving. "Native culture is not recognized and validated and at least taught, it's just silence. When Native students don't see themselves there. They don't see their people there. They don't see their culture there."

Whitewashing Native histories proved to be another strong example perpetuating the absentee narrative in East River Bend. Whitewashing is defined as "to intentionally hide some kind of wrongdoing, error or unpleasant situation—or deal with it in a way that attempts to make it seem less bad than it is" (Vocab Builder, n.d., para. 1). Galeano (2020) argued American textbooks are notorious for whitewashing history.

Galeano (2020) explains the importance of a truthful history, "The problem with whitewashing history is that it does not tell students the truth of the atrocities that Black, Indigenous and people of color have experienced" (para. 5). Students of color who learned their histories at home are not acknowledged and provided truth about their cultural histories during school. White students are taught a sanitized version of history that excludes other cultural perspectives (Janu, 2020). Some White educators failed to fully understand Native histories and their lack of awareness led to an incomplete and inaccurate curriculum. Native students and families felt invisible.

Additionally, annual field trips to a military outpost caused further harm to Native students. Educators, due to their lack of knowledge about Native history, failed to realize how *this military outpost served as a concentration camp for Native Americans*. A Tribal leader pleaded, "Stop taking the kids to [the military outpost] on a tour and make it this wonderful place. That is a military fort, when that's not what it was originally even before contact. That area was so sacred to our people. And they need to first talk about that."

Teachers entering the East River Bend school district were not well versed with Native histories. Cultural responsiveness and understanding Native histories challenged educators. Acknowledging Native identity proved critical to student success. Native students felt invisible when their identity was not recognized.

This description of Native student experiences in high school sets the stages for their entry into higher education. Native students carry their history, culture, and public-school experiences with them as they begin college. The lack of knowledge regarding Native history affects them in college classes too. In the next section, Native pedagogies offer ways to invite students to learn and support them as they end their K–12 career and begin their college journey.

NATIVE PEDAGOGIES

At the beginning of this chapter, a brief examination of the Native boarding school experience and the continuing impact was provided to reveal the trauma experienced by Native families today. The common events Native students experience in K–12 settings include (but are not limited to) navigating White-dominated environments, racism, and implicit bias in schools, and a loss of identity through lack of representation and whitewashing in the curriculum.

It is important to realize that for many Native students, their educational career has not always been easy to navigate. Native students ages 16–24 experienced a dropout rate of 15% compared to 7% of their White peers (NCES, 2008). The K–12 Native student school experience provides post-secondary educators a glimpse of the grit and resilience of Native students. In this next section, conditions and strategies for all Native students are described.

CONDITIONS ALLOWING NATIVE STUDENTS TO THRIVE

Connection and a sense of community are shared values among most Tribal Nations. Hare and Pidgeon (2011) found school communities resembling "the First nation's communities in which they lived" contributed to a sense of "friendship and kinship within the schools that created a sense of belonging, support, and respect" (p. 106).

Additionally, Wilcox (2015) determined that Native students thrived in educational settings offering curricula focused on "relationships, relevance and rigor" (p. 345). Culturally responsive schools improve Native students' morale, sense of identity, and belonging, while increasing graduation rates. Besides creating conditions for relationships and a sense of belonging, a culturally responsive curriculum proved important by giving Native students

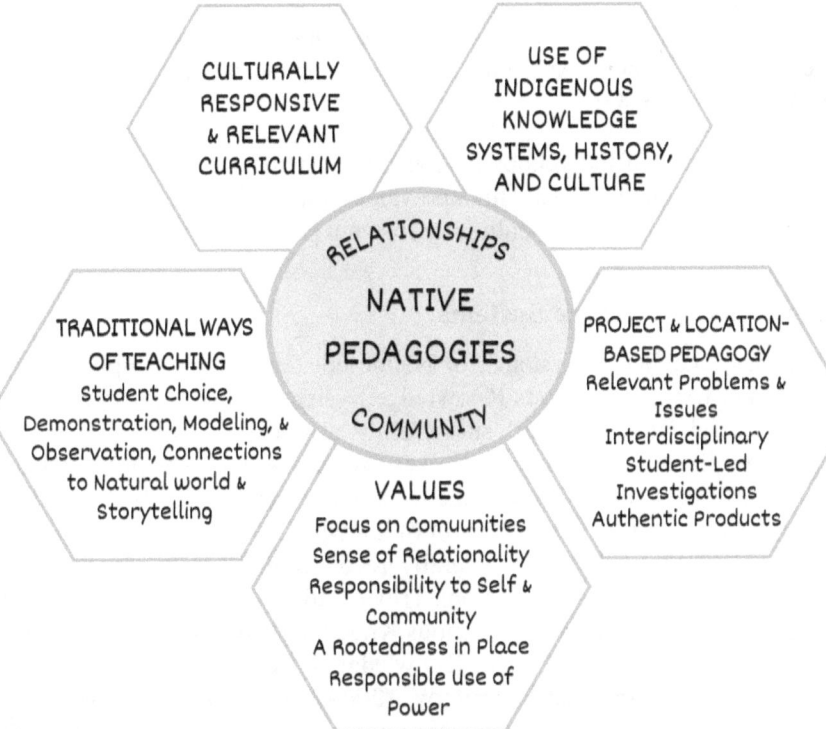

Figure 1.2. Native Pedagogies: Relationships, Community, and Traditional Ways of Teaching.
Source: Created by Jessica Jo Noonan.

higher conceptual understanding, confidence, and increased classroom participation (Kanu, 2006). See figure 1.2.

A culturally responsive curriculum acknowledges multiple cultures and perspectives within learning, instead of focusing on the dominant culture (Ladson-Billings, 2022). A culturally responsive curriculum allows students to learn more about their culture and/or allows students to demonstrate traditional knowledge systems within the learning content (Ladson-Billings, 2022). All students can learn, analyze, and synthesize information using multi-cultural perspectives and experiences.

Cultural relevance is critical. The lack of representation and cultural representation creates a loss of identity for students of color (Ladson-Billings, 2022). Culturally relevant teachers can halt the damages of traditional schooling by capitalizing on students' cultures and adopting pedagogical practices that engage student learning. Ladson-Billings (2022) explained:

> Specifically, culturally relevant teaching is a pedagogy that empowers students intellectually, socially, emotionally, and politically by using cultural referents to impart knowledge, skills, and attitudes. These cultural referents are not merely vehicles for bridging or explaining the dominant culture; they are aspects of the curriculum. (p. 88–89)

An understanding of Indigenous Knowledge Systems and traditional ways of teaching proves helpful too. This knowledge may help educators transform their curriculum by adopting culturally relevant pedagogy for Native students.

Indigenous Knowledge Systems

Indigenous Knowledge Systems, or Native epistemologies, simply put, are ways of knowing. Indigenous Knowledge Systems include the worldviews, teachings, and cultural values successfully passed down to multiple generations despite colonization efforts. Acknowledging Indigenous Knowledge Systems affirms students' experience using what they inherently know about the content as a valid and sound form of knowledge.

The United States has 574 federally recognized tribes. Cultural values, traditions, and languages vary among Tribal Nations. As such, it is important to avoid overgeneralization. Indigenous Knowledge Systems can and should work in conjunction with Western Knowledge Systems.

However, Castagno and Brayboy (2008) identified components of Indigenous Knowledge Systems shared across many Tribal Nations. These shared worldviews, teachings, and cultural values emphasized

- "a central focus on communities,

- a sense of relationality,
- notions of responsibility to self and community,
- a rootedness in place, and
- a responsible use of power." (p. 951)

It is important to not overgeneralize about Native culture or Native students. Many Native students live on Tribal land and attend Tribal schools. Smaller reservations may not have a school and will bus their Native youth to a nearby school in a neighboring town. Others, like myself, grew up in metropolitan cities and attended predominantly White school districts.

Native students' connections and access to their culture vary among each individual student. However, it is okay and safe to presume that *Native cultures value community, relationships, and land*. Native teachings and worldviews embrace the idea that we are responsible for each other and the land we are on. All things are connected to each other.

Connecting Indigenous Knowledge Systems to the curriculum has a positive impact on the Native students. Educators who connect and apply themes of power, relationships, community, responsibility, or place are engaging in culturally relevant pedagogy for Native students. These five themes are values shared within the Native community. Native students can apply and share their Indigenous knowledge to the content, thereby creating a Culturally Relevant curriculum.

Traditional Ways of Teaching

Education prior to colonization emphasized physical and cultural survival. Traditional Native pedagogy incorporated demonstration, observation, connectivity, and storytelling. Barnhardt and Kawagley (2005) explained:

> Indigenous people have had their own ways of looking at and relating to the world, the universe, and to each other. . . . Their traditional education processes were carefully constructed around observing natural processes, adapting modes of survival, obtaining sustenance from the plant and animal world, and using natural materials to make their tools and implements. All of this was made understandable through demonstration and observation accompanied by thoughtful stories in which the lessons were imbedded. (p. 10)

Indigenous people lived and survived prior to colonization in vastly different circumstances than today. However, the way Native children were taught prior to colonization is still applicable today. Instructional strategies benefiting Native students include (1) student choice, (2) modeling and observation, (3) connections to the natural world, and (4) storytelling.

Traditional western pedagogy tends to compartmentalize knowledge. For example, English language arts, mathematics, and science are taught as individual subject matters. Native pedagogy emphasizes how knowledge is connected across subject matter. To illustrate, a lesson on fish harvesting could take a western approach by studying the ecological effects from harvesting. A Native pedagogical approach could compare the ecological differences between Native harvesting and fisheries, understanding Native harvesting rights, understanding Tribal sovereignty and treaties, examining court cases involving disputes over harvesting rights, hearing narratives from multiple perspectives, and perhaps engaging in action resulting from the learning.

Project- and location-based learning are instructional strategies that naturally engage learning across multiple topics or themes. For example, a study of the Morrill Act described as "The deal—and steal—of the century," involved the price paid for land per acre in the Treaty of 1851 (Egerstrom, 2023, para. 13):

> The U.S. government paid the Dakota $2,309 in the Treaty of 1851—a paltry **$0.02 per acre**. The University of Minnesota sold those lands for **251 times that amount**. Not even the worlds [sic] most sophisticated Ponzi scheme could promise a 25,000 percent return on investment. (bold in original; para. 12)

The study of Native experience involving "location-based" pedagogy (e.g., land grab) offers opportunities to study the history, culture, and wounds carried by Indigenous people. Allowing student choice, providing multiple opportunities to observe, and incorporating storytelling helps to solidify knowledge with all learners. Building authentic relationships with students is paramount.

SUMMARY

Native pedagogy offers strategies to create more inclusive learning environments for Native students. The study of Native history is important to support Native students in K–12 and higher education. Students may be reticent to participate until they assess whether their knowledge and experiences are welcome and honored. When Native students enter college, they may be reclaiming some of the land.

If Native students attended Tribal schools, they likely benefited from an interdisciplinary approach to learning using Native knowledge systems. The public-school experience is not viewed favorably by many Native students because of the painful Tribal history and the historical and current attempts to eliminate Native language and culture. Tribal Nation histories do not appear in the curriculum.

Finally, Native students who attended school outside of the Tribal Nation and the public school system located in their community faced a different kind of challenge. Native students attending school in a Western world may hide their Native culture and values because they lack the people and resources to honor them. Strong family traditions and values support Native student identities.

The study of Native pedagogy and its implementation begins with relationships between and among teachers, students, and peers. After auditing practices in K–12, the next question grabs our attention: "What kind of college experiences support Native student identity?" The question needs answering because many Native students need to experience an education that tells a more accurate and truthful version of Native history in the "official" United States history. The Native pedagogy model provides explicit strategies for engaging Native students and promoting their academic success.

As a Native woman and educator, academic success for students of color has been my main priority. I conducted this case study about the Tribal Nation and their work with a nearby public school district. The Tribe interrupted cycles of systemic oppression due to an emphasis on education and a system of support for Native students from families, the Tribal Nation, liaisons, and school district partners. More can and should be done.

REFERENCES

Associated Press. (2022, July 25). Tribal leaders, members react to pope's apology on schools. *12News*. https://www.12news.com/article/news/regional/native-america/tribal-leaders-members-react-to-popes-apology-on-indigenous-schools/75-51a75d20-b960-48ed-a32c-3e8f2da779cd

Barnhardt, R., & Kawagley, A. O. (2005). Indigenous knowledge systems and Alaska Native ways of knowing. *Anthropology & Education Quarterly*, *36*(1), 8–23. http://www.jstor.org/stable/3651306

Boese, B. (2015, February 19). Two Owatonna students suspended for racist tweet targeting Red Wing player. *Postbulletin.com*. https://www.postbulletin.com/news/news/local/two-owatonna-students-suspended-for-racist-tweet-targeting-red-wing/article_a9a8ffcd-ec22-59c2-a724-ab298fb57611.html

Brave Heart, M. Y. H. (2000). Wakiksuyapi: Carrying the historical trauma of the Lakota. *Tulane Studies in Social Welfare (21–22)*, 245–266.

Brave Heart, M. Y. H., & DeBruyn, L. M. (1998). The American Indian holocaust: Healing historical unresolved grief. *American Indian and Alaska Native Mental Health Research, (8)2*, 56–78.

Brooks, B. (2022). Burial sites found at 53 Native American boarding schools, U.S. government says. Reuters. https://www.reuters.com/world/us/interior-dept-investigation-finds-burial-sites-53-indian-boarding-schools-2022-05-11/

Brown-Rice, K. (2013). Examining the theory of historical trauma among Native Americans. *The Professional Counselor, (3)*3, 117–130. https://doi.org/10.15241/kbr.3.3.117

Castagno, A. E., & Brayboy, B. M. J. (2008). Culturally responsive schooling for indigenous youth: A review of the literature. *Review of Educational Research*, 78(4), 941–993.

Egerstrom, L. (2023, May 5). Report looks at how U of MN was built on stolen land and resources. *The Circle: Native American News and Arts*. https://thecirclenews.org/cover-story/report-looks-at-how-u-of-mn-was-built-on-stolen-land-and-resources/#:~:text=In%20turn%2C%20researchers%20found%2C%20University%20of%20Minnesota%20sole,could%20promise%20a%2025%2C000%20percent%20return%20on%20investment.

Evans-Campbell, T. (2008). Historical trauma in American Indian/Native Alaska communities: A multilevel framework for exploring impacts on individuals, families, and communities. *Journal of Interpersonal Violence, (23)*, 316–338 https://doi.org/10.1177/0886260507312290

Galeano, L. (2020, June 16). The whitewashing of America's curriculum. *The Reporter*. https://mdcthereporter.com/the-whitewashed-educational-curriculum-of-america

Hall, E. (2022, August 19). Colleges are making tuition free for Native students. Will more students graduate? NPR. https://www.npr.org/2022/08/19/1117951085/colleges-are-making-tuition-free-for-native-students-will-more-students-graduate

Hare, J., & Pidgeon, M. (2011). The way of the warrior: Indigenous youth navigating the challenges of schooling. *Canadian Journal of Education*, 34(2), 93–111.

Humayun, H., Isaac, L. & Newton, P. (2022, July 25). The Pope went to Canada to apologize. For some indigenous school survivors, he triggered more pain. CNN. https://www.cnn.com/2022/07/25/americas/canada-indigenous-school-survivors-pope-apology-cmd-intl/index.html

Hyatt, K. (2015, February 20). Red Wing player reportedly the target of racially-charged tweets by Owatonna hoopsters. Updated February 23, 2015. *Owatonna Peoples' Press*. https://www.southernminn.com/owatonna_peoples_press/article_089d17fa-decd-5e21-86df-88810a9b7301.html?TNNoMobile

Janu, B. (2020, June 5). Race and the whitewashing history in our textbooks. https://bdjanu.medium.com/race-and-the-whitewashing-of-history-in-our-textbooks-501a15ddb181

Kanu, Y. (2006). Getting them through the college pipeline: Critical elements of instruction influencing school success among Native Canadian high school students. *Journal of Advanced Academics*, 18(1), 116–145.

Ladson-Billings, G. (2022. June, 8). *The dreamkeepers: Successful teachers of African American Children*. John Wiley & Sons.

Mejia, M. (n.d.). The U.S. history of Native American boarding schools. *The Indigenous Foundation*. https://www.theindigenousfoundation.org/articles/us-residential-schools

National Center for Education Statistics. (2008). *Figure 3.4. Percentage of noninstitutionalized 16- to 24-year-olds who were high school status dropouts, by sex and race/ethnicity: 2006*. Retrieved from https://nces.ed.gov/pubs2008/nativetrends/ind_3_4.asp

Padilla, A. M. (1994, May). Ethnic minority scholars, research, and mentoring: Current and future issues. *American Education Research Association, 23*(4), 24–27. Retrieved from http://www.jstor.org/stable/1176259

Pember, M. A. (2019, March 8). Death by civilization. https://www.theatlantic.com/education/archive/2019/03/traumatic-legacy-indian-boarding-schools/584293/

Perception Institute. (n.d.). Implicit bias. https://perception.org/research/implicit-bias/

RE Sports. (2015, February 20). Red Wing/Owatonna game mired in social media controversy. https://www.republicaneagle.com/sports/red-wing-owatonna-game-mired-in-social-media-controversy/article_f1f52fa2-464f-513d-b59d-6d1d916e9176.html

Reyhner, J. A. & Eder, J. M. O. (2004). *American Indian education: A history*. University of Oklahoma Press.

Spring, J. H. (1997). *The American school, 1642–1996* (4th ed.). McGraw-Hill.

Takaki, R. (2008). *A different mirror: A history of multicultural America*. Back Bay Books.

Vocab Builder, n.d. https://www.dictionary.com/browse/whitewash

Wilcox, K. C. (2015). Not at the expense of their culture: Graduating Native American youth from high school. *High School Journal*, 98(4), 337–352

Chapter 2

Radical Listening and Love

Introduction to Social Justice and Healing Pedagogies

Aura Wharton-Beck

Imagine a therapist who asks you (as the client) to describe something about yourself and then state the reason you made the appointment. You begin to speak, and instead of listening carefully about what you have to say, the therapist interrupts you and tells you a story about what the therapist experienced and how their experience can be used to interpret your present concerns.

The therapist's mistake seems obvious. The therapist should carefully listen to the client's story from the client's perspective and resist the impulse to talk about themselves.

You cannot get to know someone unless you listen to them—really listen to them and put aside all the thoughts in your head to focus on only one thing—the speaker's message.

Radical listening works this way too. "Radical listening" focuses on the speaker, and the listener resists interpreting the speaker's message told from the listener's worldview (Tobin, 2009). Radical listeners resist interjecting their ideas or closing their mind to the speaker's message and avoid imposing their background and ideas to interpret the speaker's message. The radical listener wants to know and hear more about your thoughts and experiences.

Like a "real" therapist, radical listeners concentrate on the speaker and their words, stance, values, and potential meanings. This kind of "radical listening," involves listening "to what a speaker . . . [says] without projecting . . . [your] own ideas and identity into the conversation. . . . [It means] hearing the kernel of an idea, and encouraging the speaker to grow that idea . . . [and understand] its value" (Tobin, 2009, para. 2). Social justice and healing do not occur in conflict and debate but rather in dialogue, which involves the willingness to be changed by another.

> Dialogue does not assume up front that people are the same, speak the same way, or are interested in the same issues. It only assumes that people are committed to a process of communication directed toward interpersonal understanding and that they hold, or are willing to develop, some degree of concern for, or interest in, and respect toward one another. (Burbles, 1993, p. 25)

The goal of radical listening is to give "voice" and learn the perspectives of those adversely affected by unjust systems. However, Freire (1990) argued "voice is not a gift. It is a democratic right. It is a human right" (p. 29). Instead of "giving" voice, teachers and professors encourage their colleagues and students to *use their voice* by engaging in dialogue and speaking truth to power.

The meaning and use of the term "radical" and "radical listening" may be associated with extremists and revolutionary ideas. However, there's another meaning of the word *radical*. The Latin meaning of the term *radical* is "root" or "foundation" (*Merriam-Webster*, n.d., Radical).

The word *radical* used here refers to a determination to get to the root causes of a problem through collaboration and dialogue, and to make the foundational changes needed to ensure social justice is served and healing takes place.

Getting to the root of a problem refers to investigating the health of systems and repairing or altering the foundation as needed. A model of "Social Justice and Healing Pedagogy" (SJHP) appears in this chapter. The model includes six different but related sectors of learning. The sectors provide opportunities to know history, the roots of discrimination and bias, and critical consciousness (see figure 2.1).

The SJHP model draws on long-standing as well as emerging methods to study how systems of oppression develop, and the harmful effects on marginalized people and communities. Ideas for lesson, unit, and/or course design, appear in this and the next chapter. The model allows room for telling not only individual stories but also the bigger stories of society and oppression.

SOCIAL JUSTICE AND HEALING PEDAGOGIES

SJHPs are organized into six primary strategies or sectors, including (1) learning about history, culture, language, and traditions; (2) investigating the roots of systemic bias and discrimination; (3) raising critical consciousness; (4) using storytelling and the arts to raise awareness of oppression and its

Figure 2.1. Social Justice and Healing Pedagogies.
Source: Created by the author.

causes; (5) identifying the wounds, culprits, and transformations (Baker-Bell, Stanbrough, & Everett, 2017); and (6) investigating critical events and its effects as well as advocating for change as leaders, activists, and allies for social justice (see figure 2.1).

While this chapter applies a model of SJHP to explore African American experiences, it may be easily applied to individuals and groups who experience *systemic bias and discrimination based on who they are instead of what they do*. The first sector, history, culture, language, and traditions, invites learners to know how the influence of the past as well as the present affects the experiences of diverse learners in K–12 and higher education.

SECTOR 1: HISTORY, CULTURE, LANGUAGE, AND TRADITIONS

Lapore (2018) acknowledged a core truth about individual and cultural identities—they pass on from one generation to the next: "The past is an inheritance, a gift, and a burden. It can't be shirked. You carry it everywhere. There's nothing for it but to get to know it" (p. xx). The cry for social justice involves knowing how history and culture affect the perceptions and experiences of people of color.

The *1619 Project* marked the 400th anniversary of the beginning of slavery in Jamestown, Virginia, where the first enslaved Africans were imported and sold (Hannah-Jones et al., 2021). Many Americans do not know the significance and lasting effects of 1619 in American history (Hannah-Jones et al., 2021). Hannah-Jones et al. drew national attention to the year 1619 and argued the first and continuous sale of enslaved Africans was a critical and historic event in American history. Yet, many do not associate 1619 with this historic and terrible event.

Teaching History

Social justice pedagogies favor the use of inquiry and experimentation over "covering the disciplinary content." The reason: using inquiry allows students to conduct their own investigations to achieve a more accurate story of history. Kelly (2014) described the benefits of inquiry and the tensions in "doing history" instead of "consuming history." Kelly stated, "I prefer a history curriculum . . . [which] questions, investigates critical issues and problems, examine evidence, and make thoughtful arguments based upon their research" (p. 2).

The content coverage versus inquiry method can be resolved by requiring students to establish the background and current reality of an issue as a necessary first step in planning a research project. Students use primary sources and avoid the published interpretations as a source for their argument.

The study of beliefs, values, actions, and ways of living for members of social groups are conducted by multidisciplinary scholars. Students are encouraged to think broadly about a project and use resources and methods from a variety of disciplines, such as anthropology and sociology.

Language binds members of a cultural group together and preserves culture and traditions. When knowledge of native language declines, the culture and preservation of the past is in danger too. Kelly (2014) described the adverse effects of not knowing ancestral history as necessary to deconstruct their experience now. Knowledge of history and culture, and the background provides students with confidence and the tools to discuss systemic bias and discrimination. The focus of this chapter is on members of the African American community.

Historical Empathy

Kohut (2020) defined historical empathy "as a way of knowing, a mode of observation and an observational vantage point . . . [used] to know and understand the people of the past by imagining, thinking, and perhaps even feeling one's way inside their experience" (p. x). Historical empathy requires educators in their role as teachers of students and teachers of disciplines to imagine the mind, hearts, decisions, and actions of people living in the past and to see, explain, and interpret past actors and actions through an empathetic lens. The voices of family and community members should be honored and included.

Empathy involves not only investigating the wound as experienced by victims but also using empathy to discover the environment and mind of those committing unspeakable wounds against others. Historical empathy does not condone the wrongs committed by others, but it studies the actions of the "culprit" by imagining the individual, social, and environmental conditions that led to the wounding. Empathy involves focusing on others and using imagination to identify their potential thoughts, emotions, actions, and ideas—using their voice humanizes the study of history.

Inquiry Versus Covering the Content

A critical study of history might involve learning about events or policies using primary source documents. One example of an historical event involves the race massacre and destruction of Black Wall Street in 1921 (Brown, 2021). Using primary source documents, students assemble evidence regarding how discriminatory practices and violent acts destroyed a prosperous Black community .

Several objections exist regarding the content and methods used to teach American history to K–12 and/or higher education students. The first major concern involves the gap in the curriculum due to the absent or inaccurate narrative regarding the experiences and contributions of all Americans, including diverse individuals and groups. The dominant narratives of history presented from a White, Eurocentric perspective leaves out the experiences and contributions of diverse people.

Another concern involves presenting history as a "settled" curriculum with no indication other interpretations are either possible or needed. This concern reveals the tensions in teaching any disciplinary content. SJHP requires students to build a case or interpretation with evidence and offer their interpretation of the topic or event.

SECTOR 2: ROOTS OF SYSTEMIC BIAS AND DISCRIMINATION

The focus on the "roots of systemic bias and discrimination" as described in this chapter addresses race as a construct and racism as a discriminatory act. The roots of racism in America dates from the initial encounters of Western and Northern Europeans with Indigenous peoples and the enslavement of Africans who arrived in colonial America in the 1600s (Coates, Ferber, & Brunsma, 2022).

> [Because] race is a social and cultural system by which we categorize people based on presumed biological differences . . . [,] race is a socially constructed concept. . . . Racism requires individuals and groups to actively engage it, grant it its powers, and facilitate its presence throughout American society. (pp. 4–5)

Racism is a structural system that oppresses groups of people and maintains institutional practices of power (Coates et al., 2022). For example, structural racism suppresses political choices, the right to vote, and creates economic barriers to home ownership.

The implementation of specific federal laws (de jure segregation) and institutional practices of de facto segregation (e.g., public housing restrictions) created barriers to diverse people, including Asian Americans, Black Americans, Indigenous people, and Latinx people in American society.

Wilkerson (2020) defined racism as a caste system and an "artificial construction, a fixed and embedded ranking of human value that set the presumed supremacy of one group against the presumed inferiority of other groups based on ancestry and often immutable traits" (p. 17). Racism remains a central part of African American history and culture as well as a source of intergenerational trauma. How does systemic bias and discrimination affect the interactions and decisions made by police? The answer to this question may be understood with the way the mind works based on studies made by cognitive psychologists.

Cognitive Bias and Decision-Making Errors

Questions are often asked regarding the police use of force and if the use of force justified the potential threat. Did the officer make a quick decision to use deadly force due to an impending threat or instead, take the time needed to assess the situation? How does the "split-second" threat and decision to shoot happen? How do strong associations and bias interfere with a reasoned judgment of a police officer and others involved in conflict?

Kahneman (2011) explained how "stereotypic associations" affect perceptions, and when combined with the need for "fast" thinking, may result in erroneous decisions—some with tragic endings. "The role of implicit bias" as a specific category of unconscious bias . . . entails potentially incorrect assumptions or inappropriate assessments about particular groups[,] such as male or minorities" (Mears et al., 2017, p. 16).

Unconscious bias lurks in the background until called upon to add to the calculus related to making quick decisions regarding what's going on and what is required. Decision-making errors may occur when a situation is not read correctly and/or available time is not used wisely to slow down the thinking process and make a more informed decision (Mears et al., 2017). How did a situation involving a young boy with a toy gun (Tamir Rice) cause Officer Loehmann to view Tamir Rice as a dangerous threat to his life? The answer might involve the "suspicion heuristic" (Richardson & Goff, 2012).

The Suspicion Heuristic

The "suspicion heuristic" explains the "predictable errors in perception, decision making, and action that may occur when individuals make judgments of criminality" (Richardson & Goff, 2012, p. 296). The argument involves the idea that a series of assumptions may rapidly lead officers down a deadly pathway. The suspicion arises out of a combination of categorizations, biases, assumptions, and associations to make a fast determination of viewing someone as a "threat."

The *suspicion heuristic* kicks into gear, causing an officer to raise a weapon and shoot or stand down, reassess, or retreat (Richardson & Goff, 2012). Unconscious bias comes to the surface through critical reflection and study with others engaged in discovering how unchallenged assumptions may harm others. While the studies in this section refer to police actions and decision errors, everyone is susceptible to making the same errors.

Kahneman (2011) investigated how potential poor decisions might be avoided with slow rather than fast thinking. Systemic bias and discrimination affect the decisions made under stress.

Mears et al. (2017) recommended the reduction of bias in general to reduce the role of how unconscious bias influences decisions, which are programmed within people due to their interactions with their family and community. What processes are involved in locating bias—in its various forms—and bringing the source of bias into focus for inspection?

The second sector of SJHP involves "systemic bias and discrimination." During the years from 2012 to 2023, the stories of some Black lives lost gained national attention due to the personal tragedy they experienced as victims of violence. The selected stories also illustrate how systemic bias and discrimination affect the Black community.

These tragic stories serve as mini-case studies for collaborative student investigation using primary source documents. The description of the circumstances and effects of these events leads to greater knowledge and understanding of what happened and why. Engaging students and faculty in learning activities increases understanding, empathy, and critical consciousness stemming from cases of systemic bias and discrimination. Tamir Rice's story appears first.

Tamir Rice

Under an overcast sky with temperatures hovering over 57 degrees, Tamir Rice played with a replica toy gun in the park adjacent to the Cudell Recreation Center in Cincinnati, Ohio ("Justice department announces," 2020). The cloudy day cast an ominous shadow as this 12-year-old lost his life just four days before the 2014 Thanksgiving Day holiday. Tamir Rice was fatally shot by Cleveland, Ohio, police officer Timothy Loehmann (Chung, 2022).

Tamir Rice played with an "airsoft pellet" toy gun in the park, after swapping a smart phone for the toy gun with a boy in school ("Justice department announces," 2020). The toy gun lacked the orange marking on the tip of the gun, identifying it as a toy instead a "real" gun. Tamir lost his life in the park because police officers viewed him as a threat, instead of a 12-year-old boy playing with a toy gun. When Officer Loehmann arrived, he fatally shot Tamir, making a two-second fatal error in judgment.

The question "Why and how does this happen?" needs some answers. Detecting biases and racism requires pattern recognition and its devastating effects on the people of color. Quite a few deaths result from a traffic stop and altercations with the police. A police officer stopped Philando Castile because his brake light was broken. The stop proved deadly for Castile and traumatizing for Castile's girlfriend and child.

Philando Castile—When Compliance Is Not Enough

Thirty-two-year-old Philando Castile stopped his 1997 white Oldsmobile sedan for a traffic stop in Falcon Heights, a suburb of Saint Paul, Minnesota. When asked to provide the officer with his driver's license and insurance card, Philando complied. According to the police dashcam recording, Philando made the following statement: "Sir, I have to tell you that I do have a firearm on me" (Bosman & Smith, 2017, para. 7).

The firearm was legally registered in Philando's name. Whatever exchange occurred between the officer and Castile, the St. Paul Public Schools food service employee was fatally wounded after the police officer fired seven shots into Castile, causing his death. Castile died at the scene and would never report to work in September.

When the officer brandished his gun, Diamond Phillips used her cell phone to record the deadly encounter with the officer and Philando's death. The recording was live streamed on Facebook and viewed by millions. In the end, the beloved and respected nutrition services assistant would be deeply missed by students and faculty.

Food for the Soul

Food serves as the vehicle to bring people together. Members of the Black community come together to mourn and make meaning of the tragic death as they share a meal at the dinner table. This tradition is an essential part of African American culture. During the height of the Civil Rights movement, eating a home-cooked meal became a frequent practice after a long day of strategic planning with grassroots organizations. Depending on the location, local celebrity chefs fired up their kitchens and prepared a delectable feast as food for the soul. For example, Chef Leah Chase fed the foot soldiers of the Civil Rights movement a community meal (Ferrand, 2014).

Leaders met in the upstairs room at Dooky's for a meal and strategy discussion (Ferrand, 2014). The strategies adopted for grassroot organizing included engaging in peaceful protests, meeting with local citizens about voting rights, or speaking from the pulpit of Black Baptist or African Methodist churches.

Continuing the Tradition

Across the country, the tradition of sharing a meal during turbulent times continues to this day. It occurs in the homes of professors, local and national politicians, and clergy. Dutta (2016) described the importance of food and cooking, connecting with community, and culture:

> I believe when we cook, we often unknowingly call on ancestral memory. This is all part of the well of information that our bodies hold and by connecting with these memories we can mend our spirit and give way to healing. The process of un-lodging these sacred memories, and therefore, sacred knowledges, is at the heart of this process. (p. 25)

Cultural foods require no explanation, apology, or excuses. You weep, remember the lost life, and you just eat.

The third sector, "raising critical consciousness," addresses the need for the critical examination regarding the development of biases and discrimination as well as uncovering biases buried beneath the surface of consciousness.

SECTOR 3: RAISING CRITICAL CONSCIOUSNESS

Raising critical consciousness involves examining underlying assumptions and biases, as part of the critical self-reflection and turning away from the self- reflection process to seeing others and injustices, and then taking action to address injustice. The three-step process increases critical consciousness because investigations start with a critical reflection of the "self." Fitzpatrick (2021) offered three basic questions to locate the source of core values, including "who we are, where we have been [and] what we have experienced" (p. 66).

Fitzpatrick (2021) argued that the method of determining shared values is possible only if a "generous thinker" interrogates their experiences and listens to the way others "define and describe their world and . . . [ask] how we might be called upon to shift our perspective" (p. 66).

While critical self-reflection is continuous, the next step contributing to an increase in critical consciousness requires a focus on others and injustices (El-Amin et al., 2017). Finally, acting for social justice should be the logical result of this effort. See figure 2.2.

El-Amin et al. (2017) defined "critical consciousness . . . [as] the ability to recognize and analyze systems of inequality and the commitment to take action against these systems" (p. 18).

Freire (1970) proposed a method of exploring differing perceptions of reality by "[1] gaining knowledge about the systems and structures that create and sustain inequity (critical analysis), [2] developing a sense of power

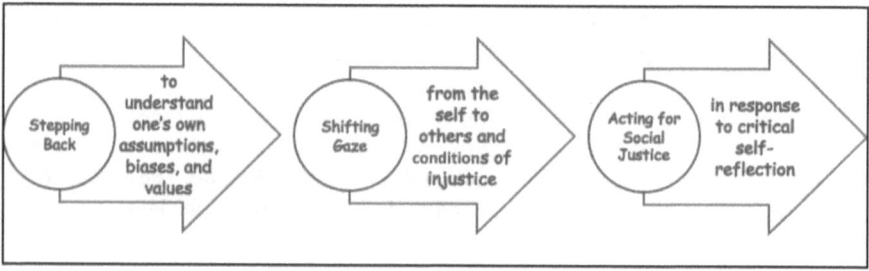

Figure 2.2. Increasing Critical Consciousness.
Source: Created by the author.

or capability (sense of agency), and [3] ultimately committing to take action against oppressive conditions (critical action)" (p. 18).

An important step in raising critical consciousness involves gaining an awareness of oppression in its many forms and challenging the assumptions about race and identity. Positionality affects the way identities influence decisions and actions, resulting in thoughts and behaviors, which seem automatic.

Awareness of positionality refers to *"having a position . . . [and] knowing* your position is important . . . [and] *naming* one's positions is vital, but *critically reflecting* on how your *havings, knowings,* and *namings* may impact your interactions with students" (Douglas & Nganga, 2013, p. 77, italics in original).

Critical self-reflection involves gaining an understanding of the underlying reasons for "automatic" and underlying biases and discriminatory actions, and then *evaluating actions with a new understanding.* "Positionality" concerns the underlying beliefs, biases, and behaviors which influence our interactions with others. Our positions often predict reactions to others—particularly during high stakes interactions. The final three sectors appear in chapter 3.

REFERENCES

Baker-Bell, A., Stanbrough, R. J., & Everett, S. (2017, January). The stories they tell: Mainstream media, pedagogies of healing, and critical media literacy. *English Education, 49*(2), 130–152.

Bosman, J., & Smith, M. (2017, June 21). Experts weigh in on video on Philando Castile shooting. *New York Times.* https://www.nytimes.com/2017/06/21/us/video-police-shooting-philando-castile-trial.html

Burbles, N. C. (1993). *Dialogue in teaching: Theory and practice.* Teacher's College Press.

Chung, C. (2022, July 11). Cleveland officer who killed Tamir Rice swiftly exits new police job. *New York Times.* https://www.nytimes.com/2022/07/07/us/tamir-rice-timothy-loehmann-pennsylvania.html.

Coates, R. D., Ferber, A. L., & Brunsma, D. L. (2022). The matrix of race: Social construction, intersectionality, and inequality. (2nd ed.). Sage Publications.

Douglas, Ty-Ron, & Nganga, C. (2013). What's radical love got to do with it: Navigating identity, pedagogy, and positionality in pre-service education. *International Journal of Critical Pedagogy, 6*(1), 58–82.

Dutta, S. (2016). *Spirits in the food: A pedagogy for cooking and healing.* Master's Thesis, Georgia State University. doi: https://doi.org/10.57709/8696135

El-Amin, A., Seider, S., Graves, D., Tamerat, J., Clark, S., Soutter, M., Johannsen, J., & Malhotra, S. (2017). Critical consciousness: A key to student achievement. *Phi Delta Kappan, 98*(5), 18–23. https://doi.org/10.1177/0031721717690360

Ferrand, C. (2014, July 3). Dooky Chase's Restaurant played key role in Civil Rights movement. *WDSU*. https://www.dookychaserestaurants.com

Fitzpatrick, K. (2021). *A generous approach to saving the university*. John Hopkins University Press.

Freire P. (1970/2018). *Pedagogy of the oppressed*: 50th anniversary edition (4th ed.) M.B. Ramos (Trans.). Bloomsbury Academic.

Hannah-Jones, N., Roper, C., Silverman, I., & Silverstein, J. (2021). *The 1619 Project: A new origin story*. One World.

Justice department announces closing of investigation into 2014 officer involved shooting in Cleveland, Ohio. (2020, December 29). *Justice News*, The United States Department of Justice. https://www.justice.gov/opa/pr/justice-department-announces-closing-investigation-2014-officer-involved-shooting-cleveland

Kahneman, D. (2011). *Thinking, fast and slow*. Farrar, Straus, & Giroux.

Kelly, T. J. (2014). *Students as investigators, teachers as researchers: Documenting a critical history pedagogy and its impact on diverse learners in a tenth-grade world history classroo*m. [Doctoral Dissertation], University of Maryland, College Park. https://drum.lib.umd.edu/bitstream/handle/1903/15170/Kelly_umd_0117E_14945.pdf?sequence=1&isAllowed=y

Kohut, T. A. (2020). *Empathy and the historical understanding of the human past*. Routledge.

Lapore, J. (2018). *These truths: A history of the United States*. W. W. Norton & Co.

Mears, D. P., Craig, M. O., Stewart, E. A., & Warren, P. Y. (2017). Thinking fast, not slow: How cognitive biases may contribute to racial disparities in the use of force in police-citizen encounters. *Journal of Criminal Justice, 53*, 12–24. https://doi.org/10.1016/j.jcrimjus.2017.09.001

Merriam-Webster. (n.d.). Radical. In *Merriam-Webster.com dictionary*. Retrieved November 23, 2022, from https://www.merriam-webster.com/dictionary/radical

Richardson, L. S., & Goff, P. A. (2012). Self-defense and the suspicion heuristic. *Iowa Law Review, 98*(1), 293–336.

Tobin, K. (2009). Tuning into others' voices: Radical listening, learning from difference, and escaping oppression. *Cultural Studies of Science Education, 4*(3), 505–511. https://doi.org/10.1007/s11422-009-9218-1

Wilkerson, I. (2020). *Caste: The origins of our discontent*. Random House.

Chapter 3

Designing Learning Activities Using Social Justice and Healing Pedagogies

Aura Wharton-Beck

One of the most common strategies used in discovering and claiming identities, locating cultural beliefs and practices, and declaring important values involves the use of story. Storytelling not only conveys meaning but it also empowers speakers and listeners to learn something about themselves after composing or listening to a story. "Stories convey what nothing else can: who we are, what we know, how we feel, the way change affects us, and our thoughts about what we should do next" (Noonan, 2007, p. 2).

When combined with radical listening, storytelling invites us to listen with goodwill toward others and show a willingness to consider others, meet their needs, and invite them into the center of the class circle as valuable members and contributors. Radical love is a type of caring in education that includes a willingness to see students through a process, ensure they learn something valuable, experience joy, develop trust in themselves and others, and feel nourished from the process of learning together. Love is a noun and a verb.

Love makes it possible to engage in dialogue: "Dialogue cannot exist, however, in the absence of a profound love for the world and for people. . . . Love is at the same time the foundation of dialogue and dialogue itself" (Freire, 2018, p. 88). Radical listening and love serve as processes as well as solutions to enact change.

Sectors 4 through 6 focus on the SJHP model; the strategies engage not only critical thinking but also the affective side of learning. Sectors 4 through 6 include (4) storytelling and the arts; (5) wounds, culprits, and transformation; and (6) critical events, leadership, the call to action, and change. The sectors serve as effective vehicles to expose injustices and inspire the call to action, causing the past and present to come into clearer focus.

SECTOR 4: STORYTELLING AND THE ARTS

Storytelling and the arts serve as vehicles to expose oppression and struggle, challenge dominant assumptions, and change minds and hearts based on the human connection. Sharing powerful stories with others serves as both a catalyst and a vehicle for change (Noonan, 2007). Telling stories engages both the teller and listener in a meaning-making process to make sense of life experiences. A central feature of talk and storytelling involves the use of metaphors. Style (1996) wrote an essay about windows and mirrors 35 years ago and educators still use this idea.

Windows and Mirrors

Style (1996) used the metaphor of "windows and mirrors" to explain how a balanced curriculum makes a connection between who and what is seen out the window (outside of the self) and the "self" who is reflected in the mirror—sometimes even hidden from the self's view without sufficient exploration. It takes both views to achieve a balanced education.

> If the student is understood as occupying a dwelling of self, education needs to enable the student to look through window frames in order to see the realities of others and into mirrors in order to see her/his own reality reflected. Knowledge of both types of framing is basic to a balanced education which is committed to affirming the essential dialectic between the self and the world. (Style, 1996, para.7)

Moving back and forth between windows and mirrors offers a chance to inspect, compare, and appreciate different perspectives with an open mind. This requires asking questions about what is seen and not seen, what perspectives in the outside world challenge or enlighten, and how the internal and external views may challenge assumptions about reality or confirm them. Storytellers use metaphors to help listeners know what they cannot otherwise understand because it is outside of their experience. The windows and mirrors metaphor works well to explain the source and tension of differing perceptions and world viewpoints.

Studies of social justice stories reveal how people listen to dominant narratives, even when they work against them. The study of story types reveals how the power of story affects perspectives and opportunities. Everyone has a story to tell. Learning how to decode the story to get at its purpose provides a critical thinking challenge—does this story promote social justice or is this someone's story to maintain the status quo? Some stories oppress, while others liberate.

Types of Stories

Bell (2020) identified four different models to analyze stories about race, including four story types: "stock, concealed, resistance, and transforming stories" (pp. 18–21). The four types of stories uniquely capture the universal themes of power, isolation, assimilation, belonging, resistance, and hope as people make meaning of their lived experiences in a racially divided United States.

Stock stories speak of tales told by the dominant group (Bell, 2020). Ironically, these stories are also embraced by marginalized and oppressed groups. Stock stories are fundamentally fashioned by the White racial frame. The second type involves concealed stories. Concealed stories capture the unspoken experiences, inequities, and narratives of oppressed individuals and groups. Interestingly, stock stories tend to ignore the concealed stories.

Resistance stories tell a powerful counter narrative to challenge stock stories (Bell, 2020). These stories speak to the indomitable spirit and resilience of oppressed people. Transforming stories serve as the foundation on which concealed, and resistance stories reside. When combined, transforming stories produce new narratives enabling marginalized groups to tell restorative narratives. Transforming stories fulfill the need to channel actions to advance the common good through productive and authentic social justice work.

The advantage of adopting Bell's (2020) "storytelling project model" involves its use as an analytical tool to detect different types of stories and their effects on people. When a "stock story" is detected, it loses its power because the story can be challenged and found to be part of a "master narrative" of power. Conversely when a concealed story is exposed, the nature and effects of race and racism, previously hidden from public view can be seen. Resistance stories galvanize action, and transformational stories change the future lives and stories of the current and next generation.

SECTOR 5: WOUNDS, CULPRITS, TRANSFORMATION, AND HEALING

To achieve social justice as an ongoing process, the "wounds" of those harmed (individuals and groups) by acts of racism need acknowledgment and healing (Baker-Bell, Stanbrough, & Everett, 2017). The process of naming the individual and systemic "culprits" who cause and participate in the wounding acts must be uncovered through education to promote healing.

According to Anderson, Saleem, and Huguley (2019), "education is needed to understand race and trauma, . . . [and] what living with racial stress and trauma looks like for Black students and their families" (p. 21). This same sentence might be written for marginalized individuals and/or groups with the change of a few words in the sentence.

Gallavan, Webster-Smith, and Dean (2012) developed a concept of the pedagogy of healing. Healing pedagogy consists of two sets of tools: "[1] tools to heal: acknowledging that the wound exists and identifying its culprit, and [2] tools to transform: responding to the wound using a tool that works to transform the conditions that led to the wound" (p. 139).

The healing pedagogy model consists of both a cognitive process requiring research and critical thinking to name the wounds and culprits as well as an empathetic process involving the feelings and emotion needed to experience transformation and change. Acknowledging the wounds of the past requires empathy.

Exploring wounds and their continuing effects on diverse learners may reveal the root causes of intergenerational trauma. However, acknowledging a wound does not heal trauma—the process of healing starts by constructing a more accurate and truthful history of oppression as a beginning point.

The tools used to access empathy as a tool for understanding the past may also applied to the study of the loss in the present. For example, the death of George Floyd became a worldwide tragedy after distribution of the video clip showing how, where, and when he died. When viewers witnessed the death of Floyd, they imagined the thoughts, emotions, and actions of Floyd beginning with his arrest and murder on the corner of 38th Street and Chicago Avenue in Minneapolis, Minnesota.

The initial focus is on the victim, and like restorative justice, the wounds require the acknowledgment of harm to people and its consequences. Students and faculty of color and allies react to the loss of Black lives with a range of emotions, including sorrow, anger, sadness, shock, disbelief, and fear of the next time another person of color loses their life. The trauma resulting from the loss of life takes its toll on students and faculty in class, hallways, on social media, in dorm spaces, and at campus meetings.

Meetings on campus addressed the trauma triggered and experienced by students and faculty with calls for social justice and change. Things fundamentally changed in education with the cumulative loss of Black lives and the increasing divides in American culture. A more deliberate course of action was needed to address the wounds created from increasing racial violence and hate crimes.

There's also an extra price to be paid; "Black friends and colleagues bemoan the fatigue that comes with not just living through such events but also feeling compelled to watch, talk about, and process those events all over again" (Anderson et al., 2019, para. 2). A few stories of Black victims of violence over the years (2012–2023) may be explained and interpreted with theories, such as historical and contemporary trauma, implicit bias and racism, and the culture of the Black community. The next story describes the tragic death of Trayvon Martin and the history of the Black Lives Matters movement in America (Harris, 2018).

Trayvon Martin: "Hooded Truths"

Noted Chicago visual artist, storyteller, and activist Candace Hunter Lee's exhibit at the South Side Community Center in Chicago, called "Hooded Truths," told a story about the untimely death of Trayvon Martin (Gandhi, 2016). Lee used "hoodies" to represent the death and oppression of African American youth. The image of the three-dimensional hoodie evokes a wave of emotions from mothers and fathers, sisters and brothers, family, and friends.

The fiber content of a simple 100% cotton overgarment strikes a chord with people of color, allies, and activists. Trayvon Martin wore a hoodie and met the "watchman" (a self-appointed vigilante) on his way home from a local grocery store in Florida (U.S. Department of Justice, 2015). The watchman determined that 17-year-old Trayvon did not belong in the gated community. An intense struggle ensued.

A shot fired by the watchman left Trayvon motionless on the ground, his eyes fixed on the constellations of the Florida sky. After a lengthy trial, the jury acquitted the watchman, finding him not guilty of the charge of second-degree murder. The watchman claimed self-defense and the jury found him not guilty of murder. However, some considered Trayvon's death as a murder and protested the jury's decision.

Trayvon's death captured the outrage of the community over the loss of Black young men and adults and a desire for justice. The Sunday church service included sermons delivered by outraged pastors about the senseless loss of Trayvon Martin and the call to action.

Sunday's Sermon: A Sacred Place for Outrage and Healing

After the death of another victim, pastors delivered resounding sermons from the pulpit on Sunday. Across the nation, Black clergy made a stand to educate the members of their congregation on the biblical and societal meaning of Black Lives Matter (Harris, 2018). The melancholy rhythm of the gospel choir called the community to act.

In the African American tradition, the mournful cadence of the call and response words between the clergy and congregation inspire action. "But human activity consists of action and reflection: it is praxis; it is transformation of the world. And as praxis, it requires theory to illuminate it. Human activity is theory and practice; it is reflection and action" (Freire, 1970/2018, p. 125).

An undeniable rhythm of weeping and outpouring of painful memories of injustice becomes the collective voice of the clergy and congregation. Beads of perspiration on the brows of participants coupled with hands raised to the heavens and punctuated rhetorical phrases like *"Why Lord?"* or *"Not another soul!"* provide evidence of the shared emotional turmoil experienced by the congregation.

The call to action led many to join conversations, participate in rallies, and become members of a social movement called Black Lives Matter. Methodist ministers in the Baltimore-Washington Conference strategically combined biblical passages and contemporary readings into a three-part series, providing context and meaning to the emerging Black Lives Matter movement (Totty & Wright, 2015).

Black Lives Matter: A Call to Action and Preservation

Members of congregations heard sermons titled, "Colorblind No More," "When Words Are Not Enough," and "Dedicated Perseverance," which addressed the impact of systemic racism on Black people (Totty & Wright, 2015, paras. 2–4). The community added Trayvon Martin's name to the long list of young Black men lost from the past to the present. Trayvon Martin's death galvanized people to join the Black Lives Matter movement, a movement that continues to focus on ending racism, discrimination, and inequality in the lives of Black people. Ending violence, demanding police reform, and seeking justice became the common denominators of the movement.

When injustice and the loss of life happens, the community rises to action, accompanied by fear—will my son be next? Trayvon Martin's death occurred in 2012 and more young Black men lost their lives during the years following his death. Every death adds another wound to intergenerational trauma because the most recent death is added to the list of all the other deaths already experienced by African Americans. The loss of life triggers a response to the wounding and the grieving process and more than one conversation at the dinner table.

The Conversation

When another senseless death occurs, deep-rooted conversations occur in Black communities. The conversations erupt at family reunions, spontaneous neighborhood gatherings, and in church. Family conversations involve warning and a protocol of how to survive an encounter with law enforcement. When driving a car, "Hold your hands firmly on the steering wheel at 10 o'clock and at 2 o'clock," and respectfully comply with police commands.

Undoubtedly, parents frantically attempt to remember the last time they had "the" conversation with their sons. The conversation is about how to survive an encounter with law enforcement or any authority figure who poses a threat to their survival. Talking to neighbors gave those who participated an opportunity to express rage and sorrow.

The Community Responds

Neighbors and family members carried the grief about the loss of another Black man at the hands of a White supremacist. They asked themselves a question, "How do we keep our children safe?" Trayvon Martin's story might serve as a launching point to examine systemic racism and discrimination through the lens of history and culture in sector 1 and storytelling in sector 4.

The after-effects of Trayvon's Martin's death left deep scars on the Black community—as fresh as the deaths of Emmet Till, Medgar Evers, George Winston Lee, Jimmie Lee Jackson, and Martin Luther King, Jr. ("Five tragic deaths," 2012, paras. 1–8). Wounds involve loss and trauma. The wound involves not only the injury, but also the assessment of loss. *Coming to Grips with Loss Theory* (Cummings, 2015) views loss in stages, including mourning and coping. Ambiguous loss theory provides two frameworks for understanding how individuals and communities might experience and cope with loss.

Coming to Grips with Loss

Cummings's (2015) model of "Coming to Grips with Loss," describes the stage in either achieving the goals leading to a healthy recovery from loss, or staying stuck, unable to manage the loss. Three goals were identified as important outcomes for the coming to grips with the loss process, to "make sense of the loss, integrate loss into ongoing life," and salvage something positive about the experience" (p. 3).

The first two phases involve discovering and assessing the loss. Next, a decision is made regarding the route—the one suffering the loss either enters "coping" or "mourning" (p. 3). The choice to mourn instead of cope simply delays the healing process. Mourning involves initial and ongoing reactions and reminiscing. Coping requires a reduction of emotion and steps to address issues or concerns (p. 3). Once the coping phase goes forward, the resolving process eventually leads to "salvaging something good from the experience" (p. 3).

A final point on the "Coming to Grips with Loss" framework involves "turning points" (Cummings, 2015, p. 3). Basically, something happens that motivates the grieving person to get unstuck and move out of a certain phase, either mourning or coping. The movement might lead to positive change or cause an individual to retreat to an earlier phase in the mourning process.

The framework describes a cycle or process for personal change. However, another loss may "trigger" the cycle to begin again—*only this time there are two losses*. The experience of the first loss may become part of the second loss with the potential to ignite and intensify the coping or mourning process.

Cummings's (2015) insightful model reveals the choices available to people managing loss. The model might provide some insight regarding the "wounds and culprits" included in the discovery and assessment of loss and the choice to cope or mourn. The choice to cope may lead to transformation and activism.

Ambiguous Loss

Another framework to examine loss involves "ambiguous loss" theory (Boss, 1999). Ambiguous loss refers to the way the loss cannot be fully defined or experienced—in some cases closure cannot be achieved. One aspect of ambiguous loss concerns the imagined future losses. For example, a premature death of a child from illness or the reckless action of another causing a death creates an ambiguous loss.

The family mourns not only the physical loss of a child but also the things they will never see or do because the child died senselessly. Parents know the death of their child is out of order and mourn the loss with each passing day. When a life is lost, the most frequent comment is "They didn't deserve to die." The statement expresses outrage but also ambiguous loss. For example, Breonna Taylor hoped to work as an emergency room technician until she lost her life in her own home—a dream cut short with an untimely death. The loss cannot ever be resolved due to the circumstances surrounding her death.

Breonna Taylor: A Dream Deferred

The University of Louisville Health Department lost a promising emergency room (ER) technician with ambitious plans to further her career in the medical field (Oppel et al., 2022, para. 25). These plans were never realized. Early in the morning of March 13, 2020, Breonna Taylor's boyfriend, Kenneth Walker, woke up to the sound of intruders entering their apartment.

Walker picked up his gun to defend his girlfriend and home (Oppel et al., 2022, para. 13).

It turns out the intruders were members of the Louisville Metropolitan Police Department. The police mistakenly went to the wrong apartment. The 26-year-old ER technician Breonna Taylor was caught in the crossfire of bullets flying as members of the Louisville police forcibly entered her apartment and began shooting. The eight bullets entering her body abruptly ended any plans Breonna had for the future.

Details surrounding the entry into the apartment of Taylor and her boyfriend revealed the no-knock entry was a case of illegal and unwarranted entry (Balko, 2020). According to her mother, Tamika Palmer, Breonna was an aspiring nurse and a former emergency medical technician (EMT; Oppel et al., 2022, para.1). Breonna Taylor earned the credentials to save lives. The irony of taking the life of someone who studies to save lives was not lost on Tamika Palmer. The death of Breonna Taylor galvanized activists and allies to call for change.

SECTOR 6: CRITICAL EVENTS: LEADERSHIP, THE CALL TO ACTION AND CHANGE

A critical event involves a moment in a time that exerts a lasting effect on people and systems, and inevitably causes change to occur. Individuals achieve transformation when their frame of reference changes, and the new frame consists of changes in assumptions, beliefs, values, and actions due to learning (Cranton, 2000). Critical events commonly shared in society are also memorable and may expose injustice, inequities, suffering, and oppression or times of radical change, which contribute to the greater good.

A critical event may serve as a quest narrative or story of change. Individuals reflect on change by creating a chronological story in personal or public memory. The story is told in three "metaphorical" chapters. The first chapter describes the status quo, which includes a statement of reality as perceived by individuals and communities before the event occurred. The second chapter describes the experience of the critical event in detail, including the specific circumstances, which explain what happened and why. The third chapter tells how individuals or systems adapted and created a new identity and purpose.

For example, four critical events inspired the call for change:

- The Black Lives Matter movement (2013) started when George Zimmerman was found not guilty of Trayvon Martin's death.
- The murder of George Floyd in 2020 was recorded on video by a citizen journalist, Darnella Frazier and distributed around the world.
- The brutal beating of Tyre Nichols in 2023 at the hands of five Black police officers took the country back to the days of Rodney King.

The call to action and protest over the continued loss of Black lives involved chants with just a few words: "Say her name," "I can't breathe," and "No justice, no peace." Activists and allies took to the streets and called for the arrest of the police officers involved. The senseless loss of Black lives provoked shock and deep grief within communities of color and allies in all parts of the city, nation, and world. The deaths became a part of the national and world conversation about race and racism.

More than any other death in recent memory, George Floyd's death in Minneapolis, Minnesota, sparked worldwide conversations about systemic racism and police brutality. Floyd's death continues to involve unresolved grief and mourning and the call to action. One officer was convicted of murder. The call to action (sector 6) included a proposed new law which bans some of the abuses found in policing (like no-knock warrants).

GEORGE FLOYD SQUARE—UNRESOLVED GRIEF AND DARK TOURISM

The intersection of 38th and Chicago in Minneapolis, Minnesota, remains sacred ground for neighbors and citizens across the world. This crime scene marked the place where George Perry Floyd lost his life. Without a permit from the City of Minneapolis, residents erected a fist sculpture, murals, and a symbolic cemetery called "Say Their Names Cemetery" within blocks of the intersection of 38th and Chicago (see https://www.minneapolis.org/support-black-lives/38th-and-chicago).

The George Floyd Square occupied an intersection, and murals and a sculpture were produced and added to the site. Visitors come to George Floyd Square to show respect and process the loss. The intersection now ranks as one of the destinations for "dark tourism," along with Ground Zero in New York city, the Auschwitz concentration camps in Poland, and Dealey Plaza in Dallas, Texas. These are a few of the places where tourists go to pay their respects and learn about the history leading up to the tragic event.

This critical event has turned into the call for change—beginning with policing and continuing with justice initiatives. I live near the intersection of 38th and Chicago. The death of George Floyd dominates our conversation and is held in our private and public memory as a critical incident, a tragic and sad event, and an organizing effort for much-needed change.

A closer inspection of sectors 1 through 3 reveals an awakening to the history and legacy of systemic bias and discrimination. Sectors 4 through 6 provide tools to communicate and acquire knowledge of past events, increase advocacy, engage in reconciliation, and demand emancipation.

The following ideas for lessons support social justice and healing pedagogies: (1) writing an open letter to a victim; (2) creating a public service announcement; (3) producing a podcast; (4) engaging in an arts immersion experience or project; (5) conducting a review of editorial cartoons or drawing an editorial cartoon; (6) participating in or writing case studies; (7) conducting an action research project; (8) producing a portrait and biography of an activist; (9) visiting and/or curating a virtual room in a museum; (10) forming and facilitating a book club; (11) researching the history behind the news; and (12) creating a collage of quotations to spark dialogue about social justice.

Students enjoy working together, tackling projects, and interpreting what they find in their investigations. The learning processes in small groups may lead to incremental transformation, "which paves the way to healing. An act of learning can be called transformative only if it involves a fundamental questioning and reordering of how one thinks or acts" (Brookfield, 2000, p. 139).

PEDAGOGIES FOR DIVERSE LEARNERS: USING THE SECTORS FOR DISCOVERY AND DEVELOPMENT

Professors and teachers can use SJHP sectors as lesson plan prompts by creating learning and teaching activities within a single sector, combining adjacent sectors, or adopting opposite sectors. The opposite sectors on the SJHP circle and sector or pie "slice" may suggest some potential ideas for lesson design. See figure 3.1.

Combining History and Culture with Storytelling and the Arts

Using the opposite sectors in the Social Justice and Healing Pedagogy circle suggests some potential ideas for lesson design. Trayvon Martin's story raises quite a few avenues of investigation. Perhaps one student team might prepare a "24-hour" timeline, attempting to fill in the details of Trayvon Martin's death by piecing together and producing an investigative report based on

Figure 3.1. Social Justice and Healing Pedagogies across Sectors.
Source: Created by author.

primary sources and news broadcasts. This might include a bird's-eye view of the neighborhood using mapping software and more.

Another group of students may wish to study the "watchman," "vigilantism," and the "rise of White supremacy," including the underlying factors influencing the watchman's decision to take a life. The culture of the community should be described. Digging into the history of violence against young African American teens and adults during a defined period in American history might prove useful in establishing a pattern of violence at the hands of citizens and law enforcement.

Another group of students might access and analyze the political cartoons on the editorial pages of newspapers or magazines as well as the commemorative art produced to honor Trayvon Martin's life. Combining the projects and presenting them to the class will certainly tell the deeper story about Trayvon Martin's death and offer opportunities to understand how racism, bias, and discrimination took Trayvon Martin's life.

A single sector also works. The arts offer an insider view of the Black experience with the goal of opening eyes, mending hearts, and awakening minds to the legacy of racism and its enduring effects through the arts.

The Arts

The arts include painting, drawing, sculpture, music, theater, literature, photography, video, film making, podcasts, posters, journals, and more. Experiencing art of any kind offers artists and viewers or participants the possibility of experiencing emotion and opening perspectives. Art offers interpretations of the past, present, and visions of the future.

Observing and experiencing art and performance involves a basic four-step process: (1) describe, (2) analyze, (3) interpret, and (4) evaluate (Lopez, n.d., para. 6). These steps guide thinking processes and the methods used to experience art, beginning with a detailed description of the art. Whether making or curating art, the viewer describes and analyzes the art form, and then interprets the art in a meaning-making process. The artist's statement may reveal the artist's process and intent whether making music or creating an object. Finally, forming an opinion about the art occurs in the evaluation process.

To practice this process, students might enter the key words "George Floyd paintings or murals around the world" in a search engine and view how various countries portray Floyd. As they interpret the arts, they may see how the artist interpreted Floyd's death. The study of art requires a two-fold examination, including the art form and its meaning, and secondly the underlying theme or statement made by the artist to the viewer.

Poetry: The Dark Villain

Gwendolyn Brooks, the first African American to receive a Pulitzer Prize for poetry, eloquently used the term "Dark Villain" to illustrate the unmitigated hatred that led to the brutal murder of 14-year-old Emmitt Till. In the poem, Brooks used the words "Dark Villain" to describe the ramifications of implicit bias and misperceptions of a Black man in this excerpt:

> The fun was disturbed, then all but nullified
> When the Dark Villain was a blackish child

> Of Fourteen, with eyes still too young to be dirty,
> And a mouth too young to have lost every reminder
> Of its infant softness. (Brooks, 1960, stanza 4)

Brooks's 1960 poem, "A Bronzeville Mother Loiters in Mississippi. Meanwhile a Mississippi Mother Burns Bacon," shows how implicit bias played a role in the death of the Dark Villain—a child of 14 years old. Although 14-year-old Emmet Till was murdered in 1955, the tragic death of Tamir Rice echoes the same loss of an innocent child.

Storytelling and the arts expose injustices and inspire the call to action causing the past and present to come into clearer focus. Exposing students to learning activities with storytelling and arts immersion allows them to see with their emotions, hearts, and minds. The senseless loss of lives, particularly lives lost for a broken taillight, a counterfeit $20 bill, or a no-knock warrant served at the wrong address widen and reopen the wounds which resist healing.

ROOTS OF SYSTEMIC BIAS AND DISCRIMINATION AND WOUNDS, CULPRITS, AND CHANGE

Returning to sectors 2 and 5, the roots of systemic bias and discrimination and wounds, culprits, and transformation have a strong connection. Based on investigations by the *New York Times*, updated on December 12, 2022, Breonna Taylor lost her life over a botched "no-knock" warrant served while Breonna and her boyfriend were in bed.

Police officers were not held responsible for Breonna Taylor's death; however, they were convicted of a crime for writing false reports about the incident. Cover-ups typically occur when conduct deviates from procedure and public safety. The wounds go deeper when those accountable evade responsibility for the death of Ms. Taylor.

El-Amin et al. (2017) studied the effects of a curriculum (content, process, product, and learning environment), which focused on developing Black students' critical consciousness and raising student achievement. Researchers found curriculum developed to raise Black students' critical consciousness involved the use of three strategies: "teaching students the language of inequality, creating space to interrogate racism, and teaching students how to take action" (para. 1).

If the word "how" was placed in front of each of the strategies, the lesson design might become easier to visualize. For example, "How do students learn the language of inequality?" "How can we create spaces to interrogate racism?" "What kind of actions might be taken to address injustice?" It's not enough to know about bias and discrimination, educators need to recognize how it works inside of each one of us.

SUMMARY

The model of Social Justice and Healing Pedagogies offers the potential to change minds and hearts by using pedagogies for diverse learners as tools for discovery and development. The Social Justice and Healing Pedagogy goals based on the American experience seeks to

- recognize the importance of history and culture in understanding systemic bias and discrimination;
- acknowledge the loss of Black lives and expose the roots of racism and its effects;
- research and experience a more truthful and accurate racial history of Black experiences, racism, and inequality in the past and present;
- experience radical listening and dialogue to gain perspective, challenge assumptions, and become more self and socially aware of racism and its effects;
- explore and apply justice and healing pedagogies to expand educational practices; and
- appreciate how empathy and compassion leads to radical love and support for human flourishing.

The goals above may be modified with a different content and emphasis. SJHPs used by professors, teachers, and students involve creating lessons that include looking back in history and culture, seeing the present with studies of the current reality, and imagining the future with social justice and healing. The six sectors found in the social justice and healing model may be applied to diverse individuals or groups to investigate their situation in society today and uncover the more truthful narrative of the American story.

REFERENCES

Anderson, R. E., Saleem, F. T., & Huguley, J. P. (2019). Choosing to see the racial stress that afflicts our Black students. *Phi Delta Kappan, 101*(3), 20–25.

Baker-Bell, A., Stanbrough, R. J., & Everett, S. (2017, January). The stories they tell: Mainstream media, pedagogies of healing, and critical media literacy. *English Education, 49*(2), 130–152.

Balko, R. (2020, June 3). The no-knock warrant for Breonna Taylor was illegal. *The Washington Post.* https://www.washingtonpost.com/opinions/2020/06/03/no-knock-warrant-breonna-taylor-was-illegal/

Bell, L. A. (2020). *Storytelling for social justice: Connecting narrative and the arts in antiracist teaching* (2nd ed.). Routledge.

Boss, P. (1999). *Ambiguous loss: Learning to live with unresolved grief.* Harvard University Press.

Brookfield, S. (2000). *Becoming a critically reflective teacher* (2nd ed.). John Wiley.

Brooks, G. (1960). *A Bronzeville mother loiters in Mississippi. Meanwhile a Mississippi mother burns bacon.* Harper.

Cranton, P. (2000). Individual differences and transformative learning. In J. Merizrow & Associates. *Learning as transformation: Critical perspectives on a theory of progress,* 181–204.

Cummings, K. (2015). *Coming to grips with loss: Normalizing the grief process.* Sense Publishers.

El-Amin, A., Seider, S., Graves, D., Tamerat, J., Clark, S., Soutter, M., Johannsen, J., & Malhotra, S. (2017). Critical consciousness: A key to student achievement. *Phi Delta Kappan, 98*(5), 18–23. https://doi.org/10.1177/0031721717690360

Five tragic deaths of the Civil Rights movement. (2012, March 1). TV One. https://tvone.tv/4513/five-tragic-deaths-of-the-civil-rights-movement/

Freire, P. (1970/2018). *The pedagogy of the oppressed: 50th anniversary edition* (4th ed.). M. B. Ramos (Trans.). Bloomsbury Academic.

Gallavan, N. P., Webster-Smith, A., & Dean, S. S. (2012). Connecting content, context, and communication in a sixth-grade social studies class through political cartoons. *The Social Studies, 103*(5), 188–191, DOI: 10.1080/00377996.2011.605644

Gandhi, A. (2016, August 31). Art exhibit reveals racial injustice with "Hooded Truths" at University YMCA. *The Daily Illini.* https://dailyillini.com/news-stories/2016/08/31/art-exhibit-reveals-racial-injustice-hooded-truths-university-ymca/

Harris, D. (2018). *Black lives matter.* ABDO Publishing.

Lopez, A. (n.d.). Analyzing artwork: Art Criticism. IB Art. https://sites.google.com/a/hbuhsd.edu/ib-art/analyzing-artwork

Noonan, S. J. (with Fish, T. L.) (2007). *Leadership through story: Diverse voices in dialogue.* Rowman & Littlefield Education.

Oppel, R. A., & Taylor, D. B., & Bogel-Burroughs, N. (2022, December 12). What to know about Breonna's death. *The New York Times.* https://www.nytimes.com/article/breonna-taylor-police.html

Style, E. (1996, Fall). Curriculum as window and mirror. *Social Science Record.* https://nationalseedproject.org/Key-SEED-Texts/curriculum-as-window-and-mirror

Totty, M. K., & Wright, V. (2015, October 22). Black Lives Matter sermon series. Baltimore—Washington Conference, United Methodist Church. https://www.bwcumc.org/article/black-lives-matter-sermon-series

U.S. Department of Justice. (2015, February 24). Federal officials close investigation Into death of Trayvon Martin [Press Release]. https://www.justice.gov/opa/pr/federal-officials-close-investigation-death-trayvon-martin

Chapter 4

The Changing Nature of Stress for Adult Learners in a Post-Pandemic World

Derrick Crim

The most rewarding moment in higher education involves seeing nontraditional adult learners graduate. Students glow with pride and gratitude at commencement, appearing as if they still cannot believe their time has finally come. Walking in unison with their cap and gowns adjusted perfectly, family members position themselves to capture the best picture of their loved ones.

Adult and nontraditional learners represent 40% of the undergraduate population and this population is expected to increase at higher rates than "traditional" students (under the age of 24 years old; CLASP, 2015). The CLASP (2015) study's title summarizes the changes in higher education with this title: "Yesterday's non-traditional student is today's traditional student."

Nontraditional adult learners juggle their role as students along with the other roles in their lives, such as parent and employee.

These challenges cause adult learners to doubt their ability to graduate, yet with encouragement, inspiration, and support, they are here. Isopahkala-Bouret (2017) identified four reasons adults return to college: "(1) opening more options in the labor market; (2) strengthening professional expertise and status; (3) giving a sense of confidence and identity; [and] (4) expanding agency to influence broader society" (pp. 23–27).

Although the four reasons are highly advantageous, nontraditional adult learners have struggled to reap the rewards of an academic degree due to the changing nature of stress in higher education. While the adult learners line up, faculty reflect on their students' stories of the pressure and anxiety they experienced to earn a degree. Graduating beats the odds of stopping out college due to the following factors: "emotional stress," "personal mental health reasons," "costs of the degree program," "the coursework was too difficult," and more (Gallup & Lumina Foundation, 2023, p. 4).

In addition to role stress, the COVID-19 pandemic added even more stress. Excessive stress reduces student progress and well-being without a way to reduce the pressure, get some help, take a break, and recharge without losing their place in line.

Adult learner stress appears differently for learners. Stress may cause students to lose confidence and feel strained by their seeming inability to complete academic tasks or reduce motivation to engage in social interactions with peers or participate in group projects. Further, stress from other living areas, such as family and employment, creep into the time available for school life, perhaps even taking more time than imagined. Meeting course deadlines and taking examinations may become too arduous. Combining these factors with the pandemic takes a toll on learners' lives.

While many people experience some type of stress during their lives, stress intensified during the pandemic. As stress intensifies, the effects of this intense pressure may lead to burnout. Burnout, the human response to excessive pressure or a prolonged response to chronic emotional and interpersonal stressors on the job, is the response to chronic stress (Maslach et al., 2001). Burnout research focuses on three main areas: "exhaustion, cynicism, and inefficacy" (p. 1).

Exhaustion or emotional exhaustion is a state of depletion and fatigue characterized by symptoms of physical and emotional depletion. Emotional depletion describes a lack of empathy and emotional distance from the clients with whom one works. Associated with both negative health outcomes and reductions in job performance, exhaustion mainly occurs from either (1) the experience of tension from emotional dissonance or (2) the draining of resources (Hochschild, 1983).

Burnout, cynicism, and inefficacy represent the key reactions to the experience of exhaustion. Cynicism, often referred to as depersonalization, involves the tendency to adopt an impersonal stance. Here, individuals detach and withdraw from others as a response to stress and burnout. Lastly, feelings of inefficacy occur when students cannot satisfy the requirements for achieving success in a course or program (Bandura, 1986). Students fear failure and avoid engagement because they do not believe they can be successful.

Feelings of incompetence may cause dedicated professionals to distance themselves from their responsibilities in response to burnout. Professionals assess the degree to which they meet professional standards by evaluating their performance using an internalized set of performance standards. When professionals fall short of the desired performance based on their own assessment, feelings of failure and burnout reduce prior gains in self-efficacy and pleasure in doing the work.

However, nontraditional adult students experienced considerable stress even before the pandemic added to their burden. Educators may not know the stressors faced by adult learners who attend classes and complete assignments along with their work and family responsibilities. Quite often students block out time to study and complete assignments but a competing responsibility may steal the time.

Students depend on the structure established by professors and experience frustration with any change to assignment dates or additional assigned work. Stress responses encompass a broad collection of multidimensional reactions. Although influenced by environmental exposures, stress responses are also influenced by a variety of other factors, such as personality, behavior, cognitive style, and early stress exposure (Harkness & Monroe, 2016).

Students with one or more factors above may struggle and experience added stress. Professors can address and appreciate the cognitive styles of students and offer more than one way to learn. Student engagement increases with interesting topics or products and choice.

This chapter examines the effect of three stress-related areas on students' lives and their academic performance, including early life trauma and other trauma-related areas, online learning challenges, and sleep deprivation.

During COVID-19, the three factors (singly or in combination) adversely affected students and their academic success, including stress, online learning, and sleep deprivation. The factors may overlap based on individual profiles. Kanai et al. (2016) studied childhood abuse and found neglect heightens three temperaments—mood swings, anxiety, and irritability—and indirectly predicted negative stress responses. Students' response to stress may intensify due to the emotional trauma already experienced.

Next, adult learners face various issues when participating in online learning through virtual classes. "Students' difficulties may include a lack of a private area within their home, inability to have someone else watch their child or parent, too close proximities with other household members, causing distractions, and domestic animals in the background" (Neuwirth et al., 2021, p.148).

In addition, there are various experience levels with technology. These legitimate concerns may explain why students are reluctant to participate in distance learning. Students often decide not to turn on their cameras, which directly impacts their psychological engagement in the virtual classroom, and this lack of attention reduces their interactive learning (Codreanu & Celik, 2013).

Finally, Becerra et al. (2022) studied the impact of the pandemic on sleep health, mental health, and physical health and found a putative effect in a

Hispanic- and minority-serving four-year public institution. Specifically, their study found participants who reported that the pandemic worsened their sleep health; they slept less than seven hours a night and reported daytime tiredness/fatigue/sleepiness.

Becerra et al.'s (2022) study found sleep losses were all associated with psychological distress and low mental health status during the pandemic. Although the pandemic brought sleep problems to light, adult learners experience sleep deprivation outside of the pandemic.

More information is provided about the three factors in this chapter along with remedies for higher education communities. Coping mechanisms and levels of support vary based on individual circumstances. Intervention strategies may reduce the distress that follows stressful encounters for adult learners and restore their strengths and well-being.

Teachers and professors can learn about trauma and its effects on students, anticipate the likelihood some students may express stress from trauma, and make some modifications. This might include making changes in learning activities and the content, creating an inclusive, supportive, and engaging learning environment, and following the recommendations of trauma informed care described later in this chapter.

TRAUMA

Nontraditional adult learners have more complex life histories than traditional students. The Substance Abuse and Mental Health Service Association ("SAMHSA's concept"; 2014) "describes trauma as a physically or emotionally harmful or life-threatening individual experience that has lasting adverse effects on the individual's functioning and mental, physical, social, emotional, or spiritual well-being" (p. 7).

In the United States, an estimated 90% of adults report having experienced at least one traumatic event in their lifetime (Kilpatrick et al., 2013). The effects of trauma may involve learners' challenges in acquiring new cognitive information and retrieving stored data, both central to learning.

Professors and teachers need to create different ways to help students process difficult content. For example, a presentation might include a memorable application of the content to student life. Practice sessions and a review of basic concepts also helps students to solidify their understanding. Students apply the concepts to their everyday experiences and spend more time learning about using different modalities to break through difficulties with knowledge acquisition and application.

Students and faculty in higher education with the experience of trauma may need an invisible shield to protect themselves as vulnerable adults. Inevitably students draw from their personal and professional experiences to make sense of the course content in discussions with their peers. These discussions may threaten traumatized students because trust requires empathy and disclosure—and the expectation of disclosure may create considerable stress.

A common factor experienced when students appear to have difficulty in cognitive processing skills may involve at least doubling the time needed to respond to a question or express a preference. On average, professors typically allow three to five seconds of "wait time" during class discussions. Adult students suffering from early childhood abuse may need ten seconds or more to consider a response or the opportunity to say "pass" until their ideas are formed and can be shared with others.

Strategies to work with students challenged with cognitive functioning involve modifying the content and increasing social contact with peers using small group learning. The most direct method involves asking students what they need. Due to these unfortunate experiences, adult learners with trauma may not learn with the same ease as their peers. As noted, trauma may derive from several factors. The following section focuses on early-life trauma and race-based traumatic stress.

TRAUMA ORIGINS

Early Life Trauma

Adverse childhood experiences (ACEs) are exposures to childhood sexual, physical, and emotional abuse, emotional and physical neglect, and growing up with related household stressors. The stressors include witnessing domestic violence, living in a home with mentally ill or substance-abusing household members, imprisoned household members, and parental discord or divorce (Centers for Disease Control and Prevention [CDC], 2019). Up to 61% of adults experienced at least one ACE from 2017 to 2018 (CDC, 2019).

Additional stressors experienced during adulthood *intensify* the effect of previous childhood adversity (Nurius et al., 2015). A segment of the individuals with trauma histories are also diagnosed with post-traumatic stress disorder (PTSD). The criterion for PTSD includes exposure to actual or threatened death, severe injury, sexual assault, intrusion symptoms, persistent avoidance, alterations in arousal, and negative alterations in cognitions and mood (American Psychiatric Association [APA], 2013).

College professors and teachers should anticipate the type of modifications needed to ensure the curriculum does not include "triggering" content. Professors foster positive and inclusive relationships to ensure all students feel a sense of belonging. Small-group learning and student choice regarding learning activities and projects increases learner engagement. Students struggling with learning may gain understanding with their peers and reduce stress with small-group learning. The small group informally serves as a patient tutor.

Stress influences academic achievement due to the drain of personal resources needed to both cope with stress as well as the energy and dedication needed to pursue a college degree. Another form of trauma involves race-based traumatic stress. This type of stress may add to the stress from early-life trauma previously described.

Race-Based Traumatic Stress

Race-based traumatic stress (RBTS) is an emotional and psychological stress response resulting from experiences of racial discrimination (Carter et al., 2013). African American students report a high frequency of experiences of a hostile racial climate (Pieterse et al., 2012).

African Americans and Latinx Americans consistently convey more experiences of racial discrimination than other racial groups (American Psychological Association [APA], 2019).

In a meta-analysis of perceived racism involving Black Americans, Pieterse et al. (2012) found racism was significantly associated with more significant psychological distress. Racism was associated with aggregated mental health symptoms as well as distress associated with trauma, such as anxiety, depression, and related symptoms (Carter et al., 2019).

The senseless deaths of Black lives due to interactions with police likely added to RBTS.

At the same time, health disparities from the COVID-19 pandemic in Black, Indigenous, and People of Color (BIPOC) communities continued these racial tensions. For many, these events caused internalized racism: "instilling racist stereotypes, values, images, and ideologies maintained by the dominant white society, leading to self-doubt, disgust, and disrespect for one's race and oneself" (Pyke, 2010, p. 553).

When students experience stress, they need the support of mental health services off and on campus. Racist incidents on campus may increase RBTS. This might include hate speech or the harassment of players on basketball courts. Professors may not know the level of student stress, but they can educate students about resources available and ensure the learning strategies and class climate support student development.

Consider the immigrant who arrives in the U.S. from a war-torn country and has experienced dreadful despair. Higher education plays a vital role in helping immigrants build a sense of belonging. School provides the hope of stabilization, a link to community services, and citizenship education for many students (Mojab & McDonald, 2001). The following trauma interventions offer classroom and teaching adaptations.

TRAUMA INTERVENTIONS FOR ADULT LEARNER EDUCATORS

Considering the relationship between trauma and adult learners, the demand for educators to understand and respond effectively is clear. The challenge with teaching traumatized adults involves providing the structure to assist students in adopting regular routines and evaluating curriculum content to look for potential "triggers," which may cause students to relive a traumatic experience. The content of a film or reading should be described and an alternative experience and/or assignment provided.

Professors announce and follow the guidelines for ensuring against harm caused by the thoughtless use of questionable materials. Teachers and faculty must see their positions as more than content specialists. Faculty must recognize the importance of the affective domain in learning and create an inclusive, positive, and student-centered learning environment. The most important factor in student success among adult learners involves positive teacher, student, and peer relationships.

Additionally, at-risk adult learners need to experience academic success early in the course to ensure their continuous engagement in learning. Several factors associated with trauma-informed care suggest ways to support students enrolled in college programs.

Trauma-Informed Care

Trauma-informed care (TIC) practices in adult education are designed to create safe learning spaces for traumatized learners by focusing on student needs, such as visibility, belonging, and achievement. An important aspect of TIC involves avoiding triggers that add to the burden of trauma. "These triggers often include situations where clients experience a lack of respect and safety and an absence of control that often mirror past traumatic experiences" (Haskell, 2012, pp. 9–10).

In TIC practice, educators likely do not know, nor should they ask students, about their experiences of trauma. Survivors decide whether and when they want to share information about their trauma. Instead of knowing the trauma details, the key to success is to find out what the greatest individual need is (e.g., affirmation, safety, acceptance, etc.) and then find ways to meet this need in the classroom (Wartenweiler, 2017).

Educators must be perceived as safe persons before they can create a safe place for others. TIC involves cognitive and affective domains. For example, creating a sense of respect and collaboration, helping people make connections, giving and receiving empathy to promote feelings of safety—to name a few. The cognitive domain creates structures for student learning and offers opportunities to make choices, establishing direction of learning, and supporting student voice and choice.

Social work scholar Dr. Janice Carello (2020) defined seven trauma-informed teaching and learning principles to help guide educators in adopting a trauma-informed approach in the classroom, which includes practice recommendations during a crisis.

These trauma-informed principles include the following:

1. physical, emotional, social, and academic respect, including acknowledging the complex crisis we are all in together;
2. trustworthiness and transparency;
3. support and connection, such as checking in and following up with students who express concerns about the crisis;
4. collaboration and mutuality;
5. empowerment, voice, and choice;
6. cultural, historical, and gender contexts that provide compassion for the range of diverse experiences and struggles; [and]
7. resilience, growth, and change. (Carello, 2020. paras. 1–6)

Trauma-informed principles offer educators various options to support students who may have different psychosocial needs during a crisis (Carello, 2020). The principles remind both teachers and students about the importance of student, teacher, and peer relationships which support a safe and positive learning environment.

Several of Carello's recommendations involve changes in professors' and teachers' roles from information givers to co-learners and collaborators with students as they make choices and produce a "professional" product. This might include a letter to the editor or a presentation of the environmental impact of waste found in the cafeteria using a PowerPoint presentation. Respect and trustworthiness include both teachers and students.

When professors let go of some of the control and encourage students to produce a unique and "professional" solution to a project, they empower and encourage students to find their voice, make choices, and collaborate with peers to create knowledge.

Teachers and professors may use the principles of TIC to audit their existing practices and select areas of emphasis based on the needs of students experiencing trauma. Based on the statistics described earlier, at least one

The Changing Nature of Stress for Adult Learners in a Post-Pandemic World

Figure 4.1. Trauma-Informed Care.
Source: Created by author; principles are primarily drawn from Carello (2020).

or more students will likely bear the experience of trauma. Another form of trauma involves race-based stress:

> Racial trauma, a form of race-based, refers to People of Color and Indigenous individuals' (POCI) reactions to dangerous events and real or perceived experiences of racial discrimination. Such experiences may include threats of harm and injury, humiliating and shaming events, and witnessing racial discrimination toward other POCI. (Comas-Diaz et al., 2019, Abstract)

This type of trauma may be experienced by POCI on a recurring basis. Unfortunately, this type of trauma continues and requires a healing process to recover from these episodes of racial trauma and find opportunities to engage in "race-based healing" (French et al., 2020).

Race-Based Healing

French et al. (2020) developed the psychology of radical healing (PRH), a theoretical framework to understand and address racism-related stress and trauma. The PRH is grounded in five anchors, including (1) "critical consciousness"; (2) "cultural authenticity and self-knowledge"; (3) radical hope and envisioning possibilities"; (4) "collectivism"; and (5) "strength and resistance" (French et al., 2020, p. 3).

Ways to develop critical consciousness involve both a self-study of underlying assumptions and ways of being in the world but also the examination of an individual's history and position first (French et al., 2020). Cultural authenticity and self-knowledge come from the study of history and culture, language, and traditions, and ways of knowing learned from other members of your culture. Radical hope and envisioning possibilities involve a type of optimism that keeps dreams alive and sustains persistence in achieving goals.

Radical hope requires courage and the support of people and institutions to ensure that the dreams of young people and adults occur. Organizing race-based healing into the categories of resistance and change revealed how the four topics in the resistance category prepare individuals to engage in race-based healing by choosing to hope and acting despite the lack of knowing what's next. Healing involves belonging as well as gaining and using the strength of the group to recover. Change is possible when people draw on the group's strength to achieve goals and take charge of their lives.

Collectivism refers to becoming and being a member of community and experiencing a sense of belonging (French et al., 2020). Two qualities needed to live "joy-filled lives" include strength and resistance, despite the existence of racism and systemic oppression (p. 3).

The recommended steps involve knowing history and culture, challenging dominant assumptions with a counter narrative of pride, "radical hope," and the determination to achieve goals. Central to the PRH framework is anti-racist pedagogy. Anti-racist pedagogy is not about simply incorporating racial content into courses. It is also about how one teaches, even in classes where race is not the subject (Phillips, 2013).

An anti-racist pedagogy begins with the faculty's awareness and self-reflection of their social position and leads to the application of knowledge gained in their teaching (Phillips, 2013). Smith et al.'s (2017) study of White faculty found they feel uncomfortable discussing race and avoided teaching about race. White faculty feared they might be viewed as incompetent due to their White privilege and lack of personal experiences as a person of color.

A method of creating a way to enter the discussion of race involves self-disclosure:

> Through self-disclosure . . . we attempt to infuse our teaching with snapshots from our own development. These snapshots and stories might include the struggles and blind spots that we remember and still encounter, influential teachers and role models and the ways in which they guided us, difficult dialogues and personal missteps, and "lightbulb" moments when new understandings were suddenly illuminated—and, of course, what we learned from all of these. (Smith et al., 2017, p. 661)

Just as White faculty work through White privilege, faculty of color work through internalized racism. Faculty of color may create harmful situations without self-reflection (Kishimoto, 2018). For example, the faculty of color's belief in the simple binary of oppressor and oppressed identities in which faculty of color are only victims and incapable of oppressing others is internalized racism too. This belief prevents a meaningful examination of how racism works.

Anti-racist pedagogy is an intentional and strategic organizing effort in which faculty incorporate anti-racist approaches into their teaching and apply anti-racist values to their various roles (Kishimoto, 2018). Becoming and being anti-racist requires humility and a commitment to confront internalized racial oppression or internalized racial superiority. Reflecting on not only how these constructions impact teaching but also how the university and community adds to the continuous process of learning about race and adopting an anti-racist pedagogy (Kishimoto, 2018).

SPIRITUAL RESPONSIVE PEDAGOGY

A neglected area of attention involves "Spiritual Responsive Pedagogy" (Lingley, 2016). The focus is on meaning, purpose, faith, love, and more. Spiritual responsive pedagogy (SRP) incorporates some of the ideas associated with anti-racist pedagogy, however, SRP promotes the pedagogical search for meaning as part of the educational process. Lingley (2016) provided a definition related to SRP pedagogical framework:

> The defining elements of spirituality . . . for the purpose of a pedagogical framework—are an engagement in a search for purpose and meaning; an orientation of faith in regard to something larger than oneself (including, but not limited to, community); a capacity for self-aware consciousness; experiences of awe, love, and transcendence; an interest in ethical or moral commitments; and a disposition of wonder and inquiry. (p. 2)

Spirituality emphasizes a sense of a greater good, shared values, and the full development of human potential (Lingley, 2016).

The constructs of "spirituality" reflect important and universal values. It draws from culturally diverse frameworks, linking spirituality, social justice, and culturally responsive pedagogy (Lerner, 2000). Adult students learn about and how to identify their place in the world, find purpose in their work, and learn how to be and become a more fully, holistically developed person (Lindholm et al., 2006).

In practice, SPR checks in with students and uses honest conversations to build a safe environment. SPR invites faculty and students to reflect on what is most important, including their life purpose and meaning, connection to others, and fundamental values. Not distracting from course content, but rather, SPR personalizes and helps students dig deeper with openness and flexibility. Faculty encourage students to see the power of education which is open to SPR. Faculty authorize students to examine what drew them into their course of study.

The potential for change or even transformation may occur during one moment of intense listening and dialogue. Students apply their learning from study and interactions with others to expand their perspectives and make meaning of their learning experiences. Effective methods of building connections with others include service learning, community-based learning, and problem-based projects. Personalization of content lessens stress, worries, or concerns and reminds students of how their investment and experiences in learning leads to growth in understanding and perspective.

SPR is a validating pedagogy that challenges higher education to be part of the lived experience. It promotes resilience while enhancing social and emotional empathy, kindness, and compassion. Students think and grow in dynamic ways while strengthening the foundation of ethical and moral life.

Being authentic, creating community, and engaging in meaning-making are core dimensions of effective teaching and learning. In summary, despite the positive reasons for returning to school, the traumatized learner has difficulty. This brief section attempted to bring attention to the range of traumatic stress symptoms learners may experience. Given the statistics, teachers and professors should consider these constructs and work to lessen the impact in the classroom and surrounding environment.

Teachers and faculty should promote TIC principles and implement counter stress-inducing pedagogical methods. This way, vulnerable adult learners receive the help needed to meet their educational goals. The next cause of adult stress involves online learning for adult learners. The experience of online learning during the pandemic only increased adult stress.

ONLINE LEARNING FOR ADULT LEARNERS

Online learning allows adult learners to manage work and family responsibilities while completing school. When examining online learning, Ilgaz and Gulbahar (2017) claimed, "Efficient usage of time and reduced educational expenses were found to be on top of the list as the most valued advantages of e-learning" (p. 46). This method also makes it possible for learners with mobility issues (e.g., people with disabilities, the elderly) and others with access limitations to reach their education goals.

Further, online education lends itself to the promotion of diversity because it is not community bound and allows other learners geographically distant to interact. However, along with its advantages are disadvantages causing stress for adult learners. Adult learners struggle to feel a genuine sense of belonging.

Lambrinidis (2014) found many students from nontraditional backgrounds lacked the confidence and technical skills to fully engage in online learning. Participants reported significantly higher levels of stress, isolation, and negative mood in the synchronous online learning experience compared to their experience in traditional on-campus learning.

The sudden shift to online learning because of COVID-19 elevated the stress level among the students and faculty because many professors and students were not prepared for online instruction. Some students and faculty bemoaned the decline in teaching, learning, and academic performance due to insufficient time to make the "pivot." Other faculty were quite familiar with online education and did not suffer the same level of distress.

Knowing and addressing the concerns of nontraditional adult learners is critical to student and faculty success. Curriculum developers partially assist adult learners through online and interactive challenges. Professors have the responsibility to create engaging learning activities in an online environment.

TEACHING ADULT LEARNERS ONLINE

Educators cannot assume adult learners prefer online learning. Student experiences may not support this preference. Adult learners may dislike the isolation that comes with online learning. It is crucial to understand what motivates and facilitates adult learners to fully engage them in the collaborative learning process and self-directed learning. Minimizing technological barriers that may interfere with online participation may require support from the instructional technology department or peers.

Teachers can feature some tutorials on the learning management systems as part of orientation to a class. Students attempt to get comfortable with the various learning management platforms, such as "Desire to Learn Brightspace," "Canvas," and "Blackboard." Adult students do not always use the resources available to help them to navigate the various systems in higher education. And often, various professors use platforms (learning management systems) differently.

One instructor may be organized and structured about platform expectations, and another instructor is not at all organized. Students may have a confusing time understanding where the content is placed and how to work through the course. Some students do not know where to ask for help. In an in-person, on-campus class, students see what their peers are doing, but online it may be hard to tell if your participation suffices.

Students may spend more time figuring out how to master an online course than the course itself. As an online adult learner, Mfon wrote about his experiences. He gives guidance to adult educators facilitating distance learning:

- Learners need to connect with you. They want to know more than the material in the text.
- They want to hear your perspectives on the subject and your thoughts on their progress.
- Deliberately open channels of communication and encourage learners to use them. (Nwabuoku, 2020, p. 187)

It is the obligation of teachers to *bridge the gap between teachers and students*. Students may feel a lack connection without the physical space of the classroom, which affords them more opportunities for connections. Teachers should develop ways to increase connections between teachers and students in the virtual environment. This includes taking advantage of synchronous class meetings and using small group rooms as a space for completing projects.

Further strategies to address challenges in online classes with adult learners include (a) "communication to reduce conflict"; (b) "building empathy"; (c) "timely feedback"; (d) "active listening"; and (e) "clear and consistent expectation" (Campbell et al., 2020, pp. 109–119). The strategies described above prove effective because the strategies address both cognitive and affective needs.

When students start a new class, they want to know the structure and assignments and have an opportunity to meet their peers using simple activities. One way to engage students in forming relationships is to pair students and ask them to interview each other with the goal of making an introduction. Quite often the partner picks out more interesting biographical content, and this reduces the time needed for the activity. After the interviews end, students introduce their partner to the large group. Everyone gets introduced by someone else.

During the pandemic, teachers moved away from the focus on content and technology to prioritize relationships. While several factors caused online learners and teachers to struggle, teachers realized the importance of nurturing relationships and changed the way they engaged with students when they "switched their priorities from content delivery and assessment, to care and compassion" (Cain et al., 2022, Theme 3: Worry, para. 4).

When teachers ensure active class participation, students feel a sense of belonging. Moreover, adult students identify engagement as a priority for improving online learning (Blieck et al., 2019). Instructors must assume the role of facilitator or guide instead of a lecturer.

To facilitate active learning online requires creativity, pre-planning, and use of the entire suite of tools available. This includes maximizing the learning management system (LMS) as well as adopting learning applications both within and outside of the LMS. The combination of tools as well as emerging technologies offer promise for student collaboration and novelty.

Online learning served as a stress point for many students due to the "pivot." The change took place in a matter of weeks. Both professors and students likely lost some sleep over how to adapt to online learning, which involved increases in screen time, and the problems of managing work, sometimes children, and school from home.

Sometimes faculty face incivility in the learners' environment. These disruptions impeded student development and well-being and negatively impacted faculty and institutions of higher education. Online academic incivility may take many forms, including rude comments, ignoring students' attempt to work with a team, and various forms of bullying. The selection of people to work together in groups should be planned by professors to ensure equity and put students in situations outside of informal social groups.

Another source of learner stress involves sleep deprivation—a significant number of adult students suffered from it even before the pandemic. A sleepless night denies the body the time to refresh and heal. The final area of stress described in this chapter involves the effects of sleep deprivation on well-being and academic learning and achievement.

SLEEP DEPRIVATION

A large body of research indicates strong associations exist between stress and sleep quality (John-Henderson et al., 2019). When you consider adult learners' roles, it would not be surprising to know that the best time for students to do their schoolwork is at night or even late at night. Adult learners often sacrifice sleep. Yet, sleep is vital to their success.

Sleep also maintains cognitive performance, centered on two fundamental processes: attention and executive functions (Garcia et al., 2021). Losing sleep impairs the brain's ability to sort and store new data. Poor sleep has been linked to deficits in problem solving, decision making, concentration, and logic—tools adult learners need (Heid, 2022).

The type and quality of sleep matters. Poor sleep quality is correlated with increased psychological and physical health complaints (Pilcher et al., 1997). The quality of sleep is revealed by measures of well-being, including a more negative affect, less satisfaction with life, and increased feelings of tension, depression, anger, fatigue, and confusion.

Prioritizing sleep is on the same level as eating well and exercising when it comes to staying healthy. One culprit for poor sleep is screen time before bed (Lombardi, 2022). Experts claim electronic devices release artificial blue light, which decreases nighttime hormones like melatonin, which is good for sleep. Doing schoolwork at bedtime reduces sleep quality because it is difficult for the brain to distinguish between workspace and rest space (Sands, 2022).

Racial and ethnic discrimination (Contrada et al., 2001) may also be associated with poor sleep. African American adult learners attending a predominantly White educational institution examined associations between discrimination and sleep quality (Fuller-Rowell et al., 2020). African American adult learners' experiences of discrimination were associated with sleep disturbance and the adverse effects of sleep deprivation. Discrimination is more pronounced among those with higher levels of internalized racism (Fuller-Rowell et al., 2020). Reducing racism and discrimination in higher education is vital for adult learners.

BRINGING SLEEP QUALITY TO HIGHER EDUCATION

The National Sleep Foundation (NSF) is committed to educating and advocating for the sleep health of the entire population, with increased emphasis on addressing the sleep health needs of vulnerable people, including racial/ethnic minorities (Hale, 2021). It is time to promote sleep health, understanding its direct correlation to mental health. Adult learners should work with wellness advisors at established school wellness hubs to keep work and devices absent from sleep time.

My vision about improvement health and well-being in higher education involves the introduction of "wellness hubs." The wellness hub is an inclusive and equitable place in higher education institutions where adult learners can come to receive information and resources on a variety of whole-person health areas. This includes education and self-knowledge; emotional support; hobbies and relaxation; and physical well-being, including exercise, nutrition, and sleep. These nonclinical spaces with a home-style design would include kiosks for referrals. Adult learners could also sit, relax, and request to speak with an advisor. Wellness hubs that promote whole person well-being should be encouraged, promoted, and become part of a culture shift.

SUMMARY

This chapter explored adult learner stress stemming from trauma, online learning, and sleep deprivation. It emphasized the complexity of learner history, including early-life trauma and race-based traumatic stress (RBTS). Stress may present challenges to achieving educational goals. As stated, an estimated 90% of adults report experienced at least one traumatic event in their lifetime (Kilpatrick et al., 2013). People of color and other marginalized populations have also faced educational and institutionalized oppression. Education institutions must implement appropriate trauma-informed practices (TIC), including affective pedagogy.

Several factors have led to the emergence of online learning, including COVID-19, mobility issues, and economics. However, studies have revealed challenges with online learning, including a lack of technical skills, isolation, and incivility. Adult learners may also be confused with aspects of the learning management platform and how to work through the course. Further, there is an absent sense of belonging as compared to on-campus, face-to-face instruction. Instructors, not technology, hold the responsibility for student engagement.

Stress affects adult learners' sleep quality. Poor sleep quality correlates with increased psychological and physical health complaints and many measures of well-being (Pilcher, 1997). Adult learners pack too much into one day, often impacting their sleep quality. Poor sleep quality also relates to racial and ethnic discrimination. It should be noted that reducing racial discrimination improves campus climate and sleep but also the enrollment, retention, and graduation rates of minority students (Wei et al., 2011).

Educational institutions must foster whole-person health by obtaining ongoing feedback and evaluating the quality of services and support provided to adult learners. During the COVID-19 pandemic, many things dramatically changed our way of life, including the experience of learning and teaching online. Adult, nontraditional learners managed the burden of stress created by life trauma, online learning challenges, and sleep deprivation to overcome these factors and graduate.

The studies show the degree and type of adverse effects of stress on adult learners even with only one factor involved, such as trauma, online learning challenges, and/or sleep deprivation. However, many adults managed more than one of the factors described here and needed support from professors, family members, friends, colleagues, and peers as well as other forms of social support to maintain their academic performance and graduate.

Several pedagogies worthy of investigation, including trauma-informed care, race-based healing, spiritually responsive pedagogy, and whole person health and well-being were described. The pedagogies emphasize strong and nurturing faculty and student relationships, identifying what students need to succeed, emphasizing and supporting various cultural, racial, ethnic, and gender identities, and getting involved in discussions of race and spirituality in "public" classes, institutions, and safe learning environments.

Returning to the rewarding moment, the commencement ceremony, you may notice the faces of the nontraditional adult learners attending their graduation. Professors, students, and families witness the glow of pride and gratitude on the faces of the graduates. During the years spent in college, faculty witnessed students' grace and accomplishment during one of the most challenging periods of their lives. We congratulate them on their achievement and welcome the next students knocking on the door of higher education.

REFERENCES

American Psychiatric Association. (2013). *Trauma- and stressor-related disorders. Diagnostic and statistical manual of mental disorders* (5th ed). American Psychiatric Association.

American Psychological Association. (2019). Stress in America: Stress and current events. Stress in America TM Survey. American Psychological Association.

Bandura, A. (1986). *Social foundations of thought and action: A social cognitive theory*. Prentice-Hall.

Becerra, M. B., Gumasana, R. J., Mitchell, J. A., Truong, J. B., & Becerra, B. J. (2022). COVID-19 pandemic related sleep and mental health disparities among students at a Hispanic and Minority-serving institution. *International Journal of Environmental Research & Public Health 19*, 6900. https://doi.org/10.3390/ijerph19116900

Blieck, Y., Kauwenberghs, K., Zhu, C., Struyven, K., Pynoo, B., & Depryck, K. (2019). Investigating the relationship between success factors and student participation in online and blended learning in adult education. *Journal of Computer Assisted Learning, 35*. https://doi.org/10.1111/jcal.12351

Cain, M., Campbell, C., & Coleman, K. (2022). "Kindness and empathy beyond all else": Challenges to professional identities of higher ducation teachers during

COVID-19 times. *The Australian Educational Researcher*, 1–19. https://doi.org/10.1007/s13384-022-00552-1

Campbell, L. O., Jones, J. T., & Lambie, G. W. (2020). Online academic incivility among adult learners. *Adult Learning, 31*(3), 109–119. https://doi-org.ezproxy.stthomas.edu/10.1177/1045159520916489

Carello, J. (2020, March). Resources for trauma-informed teaching and learning. *Resources: Bringing a trauma-informed approach to higher education.* https://traumainformedteachingblog.files.wordpress.com/2020/04/titl-general-principles-3.20.pdf

Carter, R. T., Mazzula, S., Victoria, R., Vazquez, R., Hall, S., Smith, S., Sant-Barket, S., Forsyth, J., Bazelais, K., & Williams, B. (2013). Initial development of the Race-Based Traumatic Stress Symptom Scale: Assessing the emotional impact of racism. *Psychological Trauma: Theory, Research, Practice, & Policy, 5*(1), 1–9. https://doi.org/10 .1037/a0025911

Carter, R. T., Johnson, V. E., Kirkinis, K., Roberson, K., Muchow, C., & Galgay, C. (2019). A meta-analytic review of racial discrimination: Relationships to health and culture. *Race & Social Problems, 11*(1), 15–32. https://doi.org/10.1007/s12552-018-9256-y

Centers for Disease Control and Prevention. Fast facts: Preventing adverse childhood experiences (2019). https://www.cdc.gov/violenceprevention/aces/fastfact.html

Center for Law and Social Policy (CLASP). (2015). Yesterday's non-traditional student is today's traditional student. https://www.clasp.org/sites/default/files/public/resources-and-publications/publication-1/CPES-Nontraditional-students-pdf.pdf

Codreanu, T., & Celik, C. C. (2013). Effects of webcams on multimodal interactive learning. *ReCALL, 25*(1), 30–47. https://doi.org/10.1017/S0958344012000249

Comas-Díaz, L., Hall, G. N., & Neville, H. A. (2019). Racial trauma: Theory, research, and healing: Introduction to the special issue. *American Psychologist, 74*(1), 1–5.

Contrada, R. J., Ashmore, R. D., Gary, M.L., Coups, E., Egeth, J. D. Sewell, A. E., Ewell, K., Goyal, T. (2001). Measures of ethnicity-related stress: Psychometric properties, ethnic goup differences, and associations with well-being. *Journal of Applied Social Psychology* (31) 1775–1820. https://doi.org/10.1111/j.1559-1816.2001.tb00205.x

French, B. H., Lewis, J. A., Mosley, D. V., Adames, H. Y., Chavez Duenas, N. Y., Chen, G. A., Fuller-Rowell, T. E., Nichols, O., Burrow, A. L., & Ong, A. D. (2020). Toward a psychological framework of radical healing in communities of color. *The Counseling Psychologist, 48*(1), 14-46.https://doi.org/10.1037/cdp0000342

Fuller-Rowell, T. E., Nichols, O., Burrow, A. L., & Ong, A. D. (2020). Day-to-day fluctuations in experiences of discrimination: Associations with sleep and the moderating role of internalized racism among African American college students. *Cultural Diversity and Ethnic Minority Psychology, 27*(1). https://doi.org/10.1037/cdp0000342

Gallup & Lumina Foundation. (2023). Stressed out and stopping out: The mental health crisis in higher education. https://www.gallup.com/file/analytics/472412/Lumina-State-of-Higher-Education-Mental%20Health%20Report-2023.pdf

Garcia A., Del Angel, J., Borrani J., Ramirez, C., & Valdez, P. (2021). Sleep deprivation effects on basic cognitive processes: Which components of attention, working memory, and executive functions are more susceptible to the lack of sleep? *Sleep Science, 14*(2), 107–118. https://doi.org/10.5935/1984-0063.20200049

Hale, L. (Ed). (2021). Translating sleep health science and insights to public health policy during COVID-19 and beyond. *Sleep Health Journal of the National Sleep Foundation, 7*, 415–416. https://doi.org/10.1016/j.sleh.2021.05.002 2352-7218/

Harkness, K. L. & Monroe, S. M. (2016). The assessment and measurement of adult life stress: Basic premises, operational principles, and design requirements. *Journal of Abnormal Psychology, 125* (5), 727–745. https://doi.org/10.1037/abn0000178

Haskell, L. (2012). A developmental understanding of complex trauma. In N. Poole, & L. Greaves (Eds.). *Toronto: Center for Addiction and Mental Health*, 9–27.

Heid, M. Y., (2022). What happens when we sleep. In K. Kennedy & A. Onofri (Eds). *Special edition: The power of Sleep: Sleep better, feel better, live better*, 8–15. Meredith Premium Publishing.

Hochschild, A. R. (1983). *The managed heart: Commercialization of human feeling.* University of California Press.

Ilgaz, H., & Gulbahar, Y. (2017). Why do learners choose online learning: The learners' voices. *Proceedings of the International Conference on eLearning*, 130–136. https://eric.ed.gov/?id=ED579379

Isopahkala-Bouret, U. (2017). Benefits of higher education in mid-life: A life course agency perspective. *Journal of Adult & Continuing Education, 23*(1), 15–31. https://doi.org/10.1177/1477971416672807

John-Henderson, N. A., Palmer, C. A., & Thomas, A. (2019). Life stress, sense of belonging and sleep in American Indian college students. *Sleep Health Journal of the National Sleep Foundation, 5*(4), 352–358. https://doi.org/10.1016/j.sleh.2019.04.001

Kanai, Y., Takaesu, Y., Nakai, Y., Ichiki, M., Sato, M., Matsumoto, Y., Ishikawa, J., Ono, Y., Murakoshi, A., Tanabe, H., Kusumi, I., & Inoue, T. (2016). The influence of childhood abuse, adult life events, and affective temperaments on the well-being of the general, nonclinical adult population. *Neuropsychiatric Disease & Treatment, 12*, 823–832. https://doi.org/10.2147/NDT.S100474

Kilpatrick, D. G., Resnick, H. S., Milanak, M. E., Miller, M. W., Keyes, K. M., & Friedman, M. J. (2013). National estimates of exposure to traumatic events and PTSD prevalence using DSM-IV and DSM-5 criteria. *Journal of Traumatic Stress, 26*, 537–547. https://doi.org/10.1002/jts.21848

Kishimoto, K. (2018). Anti-racist pedagogy: From faculty's self-reflection to organizing within and beyond the classroom. *Race Ethnicity & Education, 21*(4), 540–554. https://doi.org/10.1080/13613324.2016.1248824

Lambrinidis, G. (2014). Supporting online, non-traditional students through the introduction of effective e-learning tools in a pre-university tertiary enabling programme. *Journal of Higher Education Policy and Management, 36*(3), 257–267. https://doi.org/10.1080/01587919.2014.899053.

Lerner, M. (2000*). Spirit matters*. Hampton Roads.

Lindholm, J. A.; Goldberg, R., & C. Shannon (2006) The spiritual questing of professional career aspirants. *Seattle Journal for Social Justice: Pedagogy & Social Justice, 4*(2), 509–560. https://digitalcommons.law.seattleu.edu/sjsj/vol4/iss2/32

Lingley, A. (2016). Democratic foundations for spiritually responsive pedagogy. *Democracy & Education, 24*(2), 1–12. http://democracyeducationjournal.org/home/vol24/iss2/6

Lombardi, L., (2022). The power of sleep. In K. Kennedy & A. Onofri (Eds). *Special edition: The power of sleep: Sleep better, feel better, live better,* 5. Meredith Premium Publishing.

Maslach, C., Schaufeli, W. B., & Leiter, M. P. (2001). Job burnout. *Annual Review of Psychology, 52*(1), 397–422.

Mojab, S., & McDonald, S. (2001). Women, violence, and informal learning, Working paper. *Toronto: OISE*, The University of Toronto.

Neuwirth, L. S., Jovic, S., & Mukherji, B. R. (2021). Reimagining higher education during and post-COVID-19: Challenges and opportunities. *Journal of Adult & Continuing Education, 27*(2), 141–156. https://doi.org/10.1177/1477971420947738

Nurius, P., Green, S., Logan-Greene, P., Borja, S. (2015). Life course pathways of adverse childhood experiences toward adult psychological well-being: A stress process analysis. *Child Abuse & Neglect, 45*,143–153. https://doi.org/10.1016/jchiabu.2015.03.008

Nwabuoku, M. (2020). Surviving distance learning as an adult learner in higher education. *Adult Learning, 31*(4), 185–187. https://doi.org/10.1177/1045159520959469

Phillips, A. C. (2013). Perceived stress. In M. D. Gellman & J. R. Turner (Eds.) *Encyclopedia of behavioral medicine.* https://doi.org/10.1007/978-1-4419-1005-9_479

Pieterse, A. L., Neville, H. A., Todd, N. R., & Carter, R.T. (2012). Perceived racism and mental health among Black American adults: A meta-analytic review. *Journal of Counseling Psychology, 59* (1), 1–9. https://doi.org/10.1037/a0026208

Pilcher, J. J., Ginter, D. R., & Sadowsky, B. (1997). Sleep quality versus sleep quantity: Relationships between sleep and measures of health, well-being and sleepiness in college students. *Journal of Psychosomatic Research, 42*(6), 583–596.

Pyke, K. D. (2010). What is internalized racial oppression and why don't we study it? Acknowledging racism's hidden injuries. *Sociological Perspectives, 53*(4), 551–572. https://doi.org/10.1525/sop.2010.53.4.551

SAMHSA's concept of trauma and guidance for a trauma-informed approach. (2014). Substance Abuse and Mental Health Services Administration. https://store.samhsa.gov/sites/default/files/d7/priv/sma14-4884.pdf

Sands, R., (2022). Out of order. In K. Kennedy & A. Onofri (Eds). *Special edition: The power of sleep: Sleep better, feel better, live better*, 25–29. Meredith Premium Publishing.

Smith, L., Kashubeck-West, S., Payton, G., & Adams, E. (2017). White professors teaching about racism: Challenges and rewards. *The Counseling Psychologist, 45*(5), 651–668.

Wartenweiler, T. (2017). Trauma-informed adult education: An interpretative phenomenological analysis. *The Online Journal of New Horizons in Education*, 7(2), 96–106.

Wei, M., Ku, T.-Y., & Liao, K. Y.-H. (2011). Minority stress and college persistence attitudes among African American, Asian American, and Latino students: Perception of university environment as a mediator. *Cultural Diversity & Ethnic Minority Psychology*, *17*(2), 195–203. https://doi.org/10.1037/a0023359

Chapter 5

The Secret Sauce of Exemplary Educators

Gail L. Weinhold

Everyone can name *that* teacher or professor by name. *That* teacher is the one they never forget. *That* teacher did more than teach the subject matter, they made a lasting impact on their students beyond learning the content and raised the bar for other teachers following them. When asked to describe *that* teacher, the words most often used may not be skilled, knowledgeable, well organized, or even hard working. All these qualities play an important role in exemplary teaching, and teacher preparation programs emphasize the same qualities.

However, the "academic" teaching qualities leave out some essential attributes of highly effective or exemplary teachers. *That* teacher inspires words like passionate, caring, funny, creative, exciting, fun, memorable, and talented. These words showcase the elements of high emotional intelligence (Goleman, 1995), personal connection (Maxwell, 2010), and the affective domain (Krathwohl et al., 1964).

The Bill and Melinda Gates Foundation spends $500 million annually on educational reforms (Hess, 2018). When Bill Gates was asked what one thing exerted the greatest impact on the quality of education, the most important factor was the teachers themselves (Barret, 2009). Describing the implications of this study, Gates said,

> We need to identify effective behaviors [of great teachers] so we can transfer those skills to other teachers. . . . If you want your child to get the best education possible, it is more important to get him[/her] assigned to a great teacher than to a great school (as cited in Barret, 2009, p. 2).

Teachers have the greatest impact on students when they place a high priority on student-teacher relationships. This involves the affective domain that drives the emotions and moods of the students. As soon as the word "affect" or the phrase "affective domain" is brought up in higher education, eye rolls begin, and a battle ensues over the role of professors regarding social and emotional learning. Exemplary teachers pay attention to the affective elements because they know this domain serves as the "secret sauce" that engages students in learning. The most aware and engaged educators study, explore, and adopt affective domain practices.

TEACHER-STUDENT RELATIONSHIP IN K–12 AND HIGHER EDUCATION

Teacher-student relationships affect student performance in K–12 education (Roorda et al., 2011) as well as students in higher education settings (Docan-Morgan, 2011). A meta-analysis of 810 studies on the influence of affective teacher-student relationships (TSRs) and students' social engagement and achievement confirmed the positive aspects of TSRs in K–12 education (Roorda et al., 2011). "Unfortunately, relationships with teachers tend to become less positive as students grow older" (p. 515).

A disconnect exists between the need for a critical emphasis on affective teaching and a decreasing comfort level among secondary and college teachers to produce the types of positive TSRs needed to impact student engagement and learning. The 2011 meta-analysis conducted by Roorda et al. (2011) found the strongest statistical effects in terms of relationships involved those "in the higher grades" (p. 493).

Furthermore, Hargreaves (2000) argued this gap is precipitated because "secondary teaching is characterized by greater professional and physical distance leading teachers to treat emotions as intrusions in the classroom" (p. 811). When the impact of TSR has the highest potential for student engagement, it also confronts the greatest decline in use.

When it comes to TSRs at the secondary level, trust is an element of the overall classroom environment. Hoy and Tschannen-Moran (1999) identified the facets of trust, which included "benevolence, reliability, competence, honesty, and openness" (p. 184). Over time, teachers who were perceived as sensitive and highly aware of student's academic, social, and emotional needs were the most successful in terms of student engagement (Reyes et al., 2012).

When engagement extends to emotion, not just cognitive functioning, learning increases (Reyes et al., 2012). As students mature and their emotional intelligence increases, the impact of affective and emotional connections influence their sense of well-being and academic achievement. When teachers were asked about what teacher-student behaviors lead to good TSRs, the teachers focused on many affective traits (Wilkins, 2014). Teachers were quick to report affective traits, such as "engagement, respect, positive personality, humor, [and] seeing students as individuals" (Wilkins, 2014, p. 65).

Critical connection made between affective learning and emotion may be even more effective with at-risk students. Muller's (2001) case study used the extensive data of the National Longitudinal Study of 1988 to analyze the needs for at-risk students related to relationships. The results clearly pinpointed student-teacher relationships as an "especially high" need for at-risk students. At-risk students described these teachers as "interested, expected them to succeed, listened to them, praised them, and cared [about them]" (p. 241).

Higher Education Students

As students move from high school to college, TSRs continue to be very important to students' learning and performance. Hagenauer and Volet (2014) found two main dimensions of teacher-student relationships in higher education, including the affective dimension and the support dimension:

> The *affective dimension* . . . describes the bond built between students and teachers forming the basis for secure and affective positively experienced relationships. The *support dimension* . . . describes the support that must be provided through TSR for students' success at [the]university (e.g., teachers setting clear expectations, answering emails properly). (Italics in original; p. 373)

TSRs relationships may be viewed as "static," but this may fluctuate over time. The actual ever-changing flux of TSRs is affected by interactions between teachers and students. These events are described as "relational turning points" and may increase or decrease positive emotions in the class.

Relational Turning Points

Relational turning points are "one-time events" that involve the interactions between students and teachers and the impact these interactions have on teacher or student perceptions (Docan-Morgan, 2011, p. 21). Relational turning points may involve the discussion of career plans or a heated argument over whether a student engaged in deception or plagiarism.

Docan-Morgan (2011) found four distinct "relationship turning points," and called them "supracategories," including "consultation, transgression, intimation, and realization of student potential or success" (p. 20). The purpose of the turning point study was to determine how student-teacher interactions and communication affected (1) *instructor liking for students*; (2) *teacher-student interpersonal relationships*; (3) *teacher self-efficacy*; and (4) *teacher job satisfaction* (italics in the original; p. 29). Students influence teachers in similar ways teachers influence students.

A low-risk relational turning point involves consultation, which consists of "events in which the teacher consulted, provided advice, or offered guidance to the student" (Docan-Morgan, 2011, p. 29). The consultation relational turning point typically exerts a positive effect on teacher-student relationships and motivation to learn.

Transgressions involve negative emotions produced because the transgression between teacher and students may involve "rule violation, dispute, defiant behavior, or inappropriate language" (Docan-Morgan, 2011, p. 16). Intimation relational turning points involve immediate "intimate, afflictive, or highly personal exchanges by the teacher and/or the students" (p. 34). "Two categories of intimation turning points emerged, including *revelation* and *appreciation*" (italics in the original; p. 34). Revelation largely concerned some form of self-disclosure, while appreciation involved some form of gratitude expressed to the teacher.

Finally, an optimistic turning point involves the *"realization of student potential or success,"* formed from the student's description of work as well as the teacher's perceptions of student understanding (italics in original; Docan-Morgan, 2011, p. 37). Often faculty may see students' future long before students realize how to use their talents. The conversation brings pleasure to teacher and students because the students know they are seen and valued. Teachers' predictions express their belief in students and bolsters students' confidence in their abilities to do well.

Relational turning points involve a one-time event and its effects on students. Teacher confirmations may affect the ways in which the communication between teachers and students reaches a critical point where decisions get made. Statements made by teachers may result in both positive and negative turning points due to the presence of teachers who engage in either conforming or discomforting confirmation. A description of the four categories of teacher confirmation may contribute to the "relational turning points."

Teacher Confirmation

Ellis (2004) defined teacher confirmation as a transactional process by which teachers communicate to students "that cause one to feel 'endorsed,' 'recognized,' and 'acknowledged' as a unique, valuable human being" (p. 3). The power of talk makes such a difference in student engagement and the experience of belonging. Teacher confirmation "promotes students' self-efficacy, internal feelings of self-worth, and learning outcomes in the classroom" (Ellis, 2004, as cited in Goldman & Goodboy, 2014, p. 263).

A study of perceived teacher confirmation behaviors that foster or detract from affective and cognitive learning was conducted by Ellis (2004). Teacher confirmation behaviors included "(a) teachers' responses to students' questions and comments, (b) demonstrated interest in students and in their learning, (c) style of teaching, and (d) absence of general disconfirmation" (p. 3).

Positive instructional confirmations between teachers and students favor increased student academic achievement. Perceived positive teacher confirmation produced "a strong, significant predictor of learning, uniquely explaining 30% of the variance in affective learning and 18% of the variance in cognitive learning" (Goodboy & Myers, 2008, p. 160).

Teacher acts of disconfirmation discourage and reduce students' self-esteem, dignity, and personhood. Positive teachers with confirming behaviors "(a) express . . . recognition of an individual's existence, (b) acknowledge . . . a relationship of affiliation with another individual, (c) express . . . awareness of the significance or worth of another individual, and (d) endorse . . . another individual's self-experience" (p. 3). Sieburg (1985) grouped confirmation messages into three categories: "recognition," "acknowledgment," and "endorsement" (as cited in Goodboy & Myers, 2008, p. 164).

The meanings attached to each category shed light on the associated confirmation behaviors. Students feel *recognized* through teacher confirmations including "immediate behaviors such as eye contact" and engaging in two-way conversation (Sieburg, 1985, as cited in Goodboy & Myers, 2008, p. 154). When teachers communicate directly with students "in a relevant manner" without the need to adopt someone else's opinion, they experience *acknowledgment*. *Endorsement*, perhaps the most affirming confirmation, involves teachers' response to students' feelings with empathy and acceptance, recognizing the feelings expressed are "true and accurate" (p. 154).

Energetic and Active Teachers and Students

A related aspect of the affective domain involves an interesting finding: students typically adapt and mirror the teacher's actions (Houser & Waldbuesser, 2017). If teachers show energy and engage students in active and authentic learning activities, students are more likely to raise their level of participation in challenging activities, matching the teacher's enthusiasm. Teachers can raise the level of energy and participation by their actions, and conversely communicate their lack of engagement by affectively abandoning their students with their flat or depressing affect.

A study of award-winning secondary exemplary teachers found six essential tenets identified in the study as effective practices to ensure students feel valued and engaged. The tenets also appear in the higher education literature concerning effective teaching. The affective teaching strategies are then presented to show how habits and methods to foster student-faculty contact and relationships contribute to increased student interest, engagement, and learning. The six tenets reveal the knowledge, skills, and dispositions of exemplary teachers. It turns out exemplary teachers value students above content. They know relationships come first.

Affective Pedagogies

A powerful motivator for student and teacher learning involves the power of relationships for learning. Like most "to do" lists, the ideas offered in this section may resonate with a problem in practice or the continued study of pedagogy to upgrade practice.

A concerted effort to engage students using affective pedagogy involves knowing students, observing them, talking to them, and taking advantage of the opportunities for interaction. Affective pedagogies certainly involve relationships, but they also involve the way students learn and experience a class with their peers. Because interest is an emotion, affective pedagogies favor novelty, co-learning, experiments, experiences, and more. Six tenets of exemplary teaching are described next.

Tenet 1: Student Expertise

Exemplary teachers are experts in the needs, interests, and behaviors of their students. They employ key skills, such as hypersensitive observational skills, radical listening, high EQ (emotional quotient/intelligence), dedication, and their own research efforts to provide the most effective and engaging classroom environment and content. Approaches to teaching may change based upon the teachers' research.

One of the most concrete routines exemplary educators can employ to become experts in their students involves course design. There must be space for discussion, investigation into student backgrounds, and adaptation of the content to student interests (see figure 5.1). Simply repeating content based upon the syllabus from the prior term does not show attention to student expertise. It is content focused but lacks student focus.

Another way to develop student expertise is to design assignments and assessments that not only give students opportunities to show their knowledge of the content but also provide the educator with content for research on the students. For example, assignments that give students the choice to compare or contrast the content to their own experiences or examples will result in work that shows academic progress and gives an opportunity for

Figure 5.1. Affective Pedagogies.
Source: Created by Jessica Jo Noonan.

heightened student expertise acquired by the professor or teacher during the evaluation of assignments.

Creating space for in-the-moment adaption is also a best practice to allow for radical listening. Consider what ways students share their thoughts with professors or teachers. Are their multiple modes for students to speak, write, and record content? Furthermore, are students given opportunities to make personal connections, share extensions of the content beyond the examples given by the teacher, and speak about their struggles?

An exemplary affective educator must consider how they can make space for radical listening if teacher talk dominates the class. Currently the focus of work on emotional intelligence (EQ) has been limited to business and leadership. The focus on developing emotional intelligence might be emphasized in student learning, but no mention might be made of the teacher's emotional intelligence.

Until now, the research has been focused on improving the social-emotional skills of students, when those who teach those skills may have little or no training or low EQ themselves. EQ can be and *is* taught in other professions. Now it needs to be taught to future and current teachers and professors because the data clearly support the value of the EQ needed to learn about their students—including their background, interests, and future.

Tenet 2: Relationship Development

Expert teachers not only know the immense value of student-faculty relationships, but they also know how to make them happen. This is a skill all educators can learn and apply. It begins with a relationship focus as the priority for each year or term. This relationship, however, is heightened and even accelerated by involvement with students outside the classroom. Finally, to really build that transcended level of relationships, exemplary teachers are not afraid to love and build trust. These top teachers know the deeper and more genuine the relationship, the more successful the learning.

One of the ways to assure relationship development and trust is involvement outside the classroom. This can be literal, as in the halls, and was also referred to as making "appearances" at extracurricular events, inviting a student to your office for coffee, or really maximizing advising time to go beyond academic success.

Although very nontraditional in university courses, it is also possible to shake things up by greeting students at the door or going around the room before class begins to check in with students rather than setting up technology or reviewing notes. These intentional but unscripted moments make individual students feel seen and valued beyond their performance in class.

Exemplary teachers take their relationships to a much deeper and intentional level. It begins on day one, moves in and out of the classroom, involves love and trust, and transcends what students expect from their teachers. To have a transcendent relationship with students, teachers must exceed their expectations and overcome their doubts. This is built over time and much like the characterization level of the affective domain (Krathwohl et al., 1964), it is a level often aimed for but very difficult to achieve.

Evidence that this elite level has been achieved may be a heart-felt letter given at the end of the year from a student who is struggling to say goodbye or a genuine thank-you from a grateful student. These give a teacher confirmation of the true effects of their teaching. The most obvious recommendation to current classroom professors and teachers is to create an honest assessment of how deep their relationships with students really go.

As one teacher put it, "All teachers know that relationships are important, but you're about a different level." An analogy for this could come from music. Some pieces are light, fun, and easy to listen to. Then there are others that transport, evoke strong emotions, and take on a special place in the heart and mind of the listener. Like music, exemplary teachers create transcendent relationships that evoke just as much power.

One way to access TSRs is obvious but rare—ask the students themselves. Consider giving students an exit card to describe their experience, complete an online survey (anonymous) with questions about their experience of the class, or pose a question to answer on an actual or virtual sticky note.

One of the most powerful questions an educator can ask their students, well before the final evaluation, is "How can I be a better teacher for you?" or "What is something about you that I should know?" The first should allow students to answer anonymously, while the second purposefully looks to get specific relationship building information from each student.

Tenet 3: Teaching Valued Above Content

Exemplary teachers will put aside the content to teach the lesson. These teachers recognize teaching the whole student may require a change in the lesson plan. The content is a vehicle for learning, but the development of the individual is the true goal. The implications of this are significant for both current and preservice teachers. The focus on what one teaches must be secondary to whom one teaches.

Exemplary teachers know how to show rather than tell. This is evidenced in their storytelling prowess when they often answer questions with a memorable narrative. As evidenced back to the time of biblical parables, professors and teachers know how to use the art of storytelling to engage the brain and emotions. Storytelling ignites not only the cognitive but also the emotional centers of the brain and improves long-term memory.

Furthermore, professors need to have the confidence to put down the lesson plan and teach without having to repeatedly glance at their notes. If a teacher is focused on getting through the agenda on the board or slides in the presentation, they may often miss the cues students are sending to them. When teaching is valued above content, an exemplary educator is aware of and engaged with the audience.

As a university field supervisor and faculty development director, I often conduct classroom observations. When I see professors and teachers begin their lessons with immediate academic content, I know they missed an opportunity to solidify relationships through student-to-teacher and student-to-student contact. If starting with academic content is routine—no greeting or conversation with students—the practice largely ignores the human condition.

Instead, teachers need to look at student readiness to learn through the lens of the student and consider the following:

- Where did they just come from and what are they probably thinking about?
- Why should they care about this?
- How do I get them interested and thinking about what we are going to talk about today?
- How does this connect to their world right now?

Exemplary teachers are quite easy to spot in this situation. They begin class by connecting to the students, hooking them in with a powerful question, discussion, video, or even a real-world example they know will pique their interest. Then they expertly channel student interest to segue into the content. Exemplary professors and teachers emphasize "a student-centered beginning" to engage students before jumping into the content.

Intentional, crafted, planned, and thought-provoking closures at the end of class make such a big difference. In my observations of educators at all stages, the piece that often gets the least amount of time and preparation is the closure of a class. What should be the grand finale of the day is too often a race to get in last minute instructions or assignment details. Instead, exemplary professors and teachers thoughtfully execute a carefully crafted closure that answers the "so what" of the day. Teachers should consider, "So what do I want my students thinking, feeling, remembering as they leave today?"

The primacy/recency effect in cognitive psychology (Jahnke, 1965) posits that our brains remember best what is presented first (primacy), that is, the tendency to remember the most recently presented information best (recency). Educators need to consider very carefully and thoughtfully what they present first and last in any lesson.

In terms of building relationships and trust, one of the ways students gain respect for what they learn in the class is by thoughtfully considering what the content means to them and what is in it for them. An exemplary teacher can give this "so what" thinking and plan it in a way that reminds them not only of the importance of what they covered that day but also the relevancy it has to them now and in the future.

The challenge is to not let the clock run out and skip the closure step. When teaching is valued above content, an exemplary teacher knows if they end in haste, it is just a waste. As corny as that may sound, the sentiment is substantiated. Ask a student about class that day, and if the closure was done well, they can recall the "so what." What they share shows how they internalized the message from the teacher and how well they recognized their efforts to connect on a very human level. Bonus—it often leads to higher course evaluations and qualitative feedback as well!

Tenet 4: Engagement and Energy

The classroom of an exemplary teacher has a buzz and an energy to it. Students naturally respond to the energy and attitude of their teacher. Exemplary teachers know how to use this naturally empathetic response to improve the classroom environment and increase engagement. These teachers recognize they must bring it every day and they must have the ability to turn it on from the moment they step into a room. Their classroom reflects their own passion and excitement for teaching and learning.

The issue with words like "magic" and "vibe" contributes to the misconception that they cannot be captured and taught. Teachers can inspire other teachers, but there is rarely the opportunity to visit each other's classrooms. This is something that faculty members can change by creating a culture of collaboration and peer observation. One of my favorite comments from students on exit cards I give in my classes is "I was always excited for class because I never knew what we were going to do that day."

Although some routine practices provide comfort, how the learning happens and what a professor does to present that content can and needs to be varied to improve student engagement. Addressing various learning styles and engaging different kinds of presentations helps to keep learners plugged in and on their toes. One of my university mentors, Jerilyn Bach, once said, "If the students aren't learning then you aren't really teaching." What this implies is that just because one gets up in a classroom and presents, it does not mean they are teaching. Teaching requires engagement and active learning.

In the exemplary teacher's classroom, engagement comes naturally because the students are responding to the energy and passion of the teacher, and they feel their place in that class is valued. As adult learners, one of the greatest desires is to have choice and ownership in their work. Professors can provide more intrinsic motivation by offering students choices in their course. Some recommendations for this include multiple options and modes of delivery for assignments. If the objectives are met, why must the product be the same? Instead, professors can at times give students the choice to show their learning in their own way.

Another way to increase engagement and energy in the classroom is to provide an audience other than just the professor. Exemplary educators should look at their key assessments and identify an authentic audience outside the classroom. Professors can also have this key conversation with students to help with relationship building and connection at the beginning of the term.

Keep in mind that if something is engaging and thought-provoking, it is not difficult to get participants to jump into the work. To improve this in classrooms, one of the most important questions professors and teachers need to ask themselves is "Would I want to be a student in this classroom today?"

Also, answer honestly, "Would I be interested in what we are doing right now?" Most importantly, when educators invest energy into their students, they see that energy come back. It comes back in student engagement, in their work, their attitude, and the energy they pour into their teacher. Professors invest in students because if they do not see results, they drain their own capacity to keep up the very hard work of teaching.

Tenet 5: Teacher Humility and Transparency

Although there is some doubt to its origin, the wisdom paradox posits that the more one knows, the more they realize how little they know. As lifelong learners and dedicated professionals, exemplary teachers in many ways echo this belief. They realize that because the students and the world are always changing, learning never stops, and teaching is ever striving to adapt. It is this strive for excellence that brings with it mistakes, risk, and vulnerability.

Affective, exemplary educators model the process of learning, which means they are open about their mistakes but also always working to become better. To become a teacher of humility and transparency, one must keep striving for improvement and trying new things. One of the best ways to inspire this is by studying good teachers and communicators. The fastest way to callous indifference is to stop getting inspired. That is why universities should provide more time and opportunities for faculty to observe other faculty and learn from them.

Teacher learning often happens through observation of master teachers. The opportunity to observe effective teaching motivates educators to upgrade their practice. Teaching with a top group of hard-working teachers and professors raises the expectations of those joining a new department or school. Some teachers get "star" billing. Being a part of the department pushes and inspires colleagues. Sometimes the observation discourages teachers and professors because they compare their development to the observed teacher and recognize how they fall short.

Eventually professors find a way to be successful by figuring out what they do well and leveraging this new knowledge to learn more. The more professors focus on students and less on themselves, the more they will likely love their job and their students. Exemplary educators remain humble not only because they know they are always a work in progress but also because they know the real stars are the students and the future they hold.

Tenet 6: Teacher Movement

Exemplary teachers are multitasking ninjas, and they use the whole body to really engage every student. Teaching is an active sport and exemplary teachers use movement to communicate and facilitate learning in every inch of the room. Movement is an activator and whether it is taking a seat right in the center of the action or carouseling around the room like a conductor, the exemplary professor moves with purpose.

University funding for classroom technology and even room layout needs to change in a post COVID-19 world. The global pandemic has forced schools to provide both online and seated instruction and many of these shifts may continue as demand for more alternative educational options and accommodations increase. As such, professors cannot be stuck at a computer station or limited to a small camera frame. Positive classroom movement requires technological funding to create classrooms that can thrive across platforms.

As school design adapts and improves post-pandemic, universities should consider a move away from the panoptic structure of control to more open spaces, cozy nooks, colorful layouts, break out movement areas, and more flexible seating. If most adults had to sit at a small, plastic desk for several hours a day, this change would have already occurred. This again highlights those exemplary educators who consider learning from the perspective of the students and adapt to create environments to inspire rather than contain.

Movement includes the use of gestures, facial expressions, and physical movement around the room. One might think this is innate, but my experience in observing preservice and new teachers is that often they get "stuck" up front by their materials and equipment because they do not have the confidence in their content enough to move away and because they are still somewhat intimidated by their students.

Once relationships are developed and their content confidence improves, movement usually also increases. The message in this is clear: exemplary teachers move in part because they have mastered their content but also because they want to be a part of the room and interact with their students rather than remain distant from them.

If a professor gets too comfortable at a podium, put a sticky note on their notes or computer that simply says, "MOVE!" And if low energy is a cause for taking a seat, keep in mind that energy is very contagious. Just as students will respond to their teachers' energy levels, teachers can also benefit from the energy given off by their students when they are engaged and participating actively in the lesson. One of the best energizers for teachers is when the room is abuzz with participation and genuine engagement. In that environment, exemplary professors thrive and refuel their passion for what they do.

Professors can also foster movement through classroom collaboration. For example, teachers can mix up student groups, whom they sit by, and the classmates they often partner with in discussion. Number students off for different activities starting in different parts of the room each time. Online teachers can manually assign students to small groups to expand peer relationships. This combines movement and collaboration where both teachers and students are interacting and learning from and about each other.

Proximity of the professor to the students is also a key area for change or improvement. There needs to be opportunities for professors to interact and engage with students individually and within their proximity to each class. This may not only improve their engagement, but also improve the relationship between students and build a classroom community.

On a much more emotional level, proximity is a necessary and powerful element of the human condition. More than ever in this generation, this has become very apparent and painfully real as social distancing became the primary defense against COVID-19 during the pandemic. The very act of meeting face-to-face, making natural and/or culturally appropriate eye contact, and sitting in physical proximity to each other nourishes our emotional well-being. One need only to refer to research on infant mortality that show babies deprived of physical touch; here we see overwhelming evidence that humans crave and need proximity to other individuals to avoid cognitive delay, decline, or even death due to a "lack of love" (Vareia-Silva, 2016, para. 4).

There is power in a supportive pat on the back, high-five, elbow bump, or much-needed applause. Exemplary teachers not only know this, but they also crave it themselves. One element of education this pandemic has uncovered is that although students can be taught online, they more often thrive with in-person connection, movement, and proximity (Kamenetz, 2020).

For most students and faculty, the human condition of teaching and learning cannot be replaced by a screen. Engagement thrives in proximity with genuine emotion where all the verbal and nonverbal information on full display.

However, difficult times may once again require a paradigm shift in the way we deliver content—often referred to as the "pivot" to online learning. Course design, management of technology, and more took away professors' attention to students' social and emotional needs. *If another pivot is needed to online learning, the pivot must first and foremost involve the need for student and faculty contact and the building of trust and relationships.* This fuels student engagement and learning and helps students and faculty manage in difficult times.

SUMMARY

The "secret sauce" of exemplary educators is really no secret. In fact, it is something everyone recognizes but we struggle to articulate. Patience (2008) emphasized the importance of intellect and emotion in the ability to participate in democratic cultures:

Democratic citizenship . . . requires informed people with well-developed capacities to cooperate sympathetically, tolerantly and with understanding across a wide range of cultural, religious, language and gender barriers. To achieve this . . . [democratic citizens] need to embrace the human experience in all its complexities and possibilities. . . . Affective pedagogy is as much about feelings and emotions as it is about learning outcomes. Indeed, the feelings and emotions are inseparable from the learning outcomes. (p. 59)

Noticing and valuing the importance of getting to know students well and using this knowledge to create a more engaging learning environment raises the motivation level of most students. Emphasizing student teacher contact enhances everyone's experience. Using the practices of affective teaching in all the domains support student and teacher growth.

REFERENCES

Barret, V. (2009, January 26). Bill Gates: It's the teacher, stupid. *Forbes.* https://www.forbes.com/2009/01/26/bill-gates-letter-tech-enter-cz_vb_0126billgates.html

Docan-Morgan, T. (2011). "Everything changed": Relational turning point events in college teacher–student relationships from teachers' perspectives. *Communication Education,* 60 (1), 20–50, DOI: 10.1080/03634523.2010.497223

Ellis, K. (2004). The impact of perceived teacher confirmation on receiver apprehension, motivation, and learning. *Communication Education,* 53(1), 1–20. https://doi-org.ezproxy.stthomas.edu/10.1080/0363452032000135742

Goldman, Z. W., & Goodboy, A. K. (2014). Making students feel better: Examining the relationships between teacher confirmation and college students' emotionnal outcomes, *Communication Education,* (3) 63, 259–277, DOI: 10.1080/03634523.2014.920091

Goleman, D. (1995). *Emotional intelligence.* Bantam Books.

Goodboy, A. K., & Myers, S. A. (2008). The effect of teacher confirmation on student communication and learning outcomes. *Communication Education,* 57(2), 153–179.

Hagenauer, G., & Volet, S. E. (2014). Teacher–student relationship at university: An important yet under-researched field, *Oxford Review of Education,* 40(3), 370–388, DOI: 10.1080/03054985.2014.921613

Hargreaves, A. (2000). Mixed emotions: Teachers' perceptions of their interactions with students. *Teaching and Teacher Education,* 16(8) 811–826. https://doi.org/10.1016/S0742-051X(00)00028-7

Hess, A. J. (2018, February 14). Bill and Melinda Gates have spent billions on US education, but haven't seem as much progress as they'd like. *CNBC.* https://www.cnbc.com/2018/02/13/bill-and-melinda-gates-have-spent-billions-on-us-education-initiatives.html

Houser, M. L., & Waldbuesser, C. (2017). Emotional contagion in the classroom: The impact of teacher satisfaction and confirmation on perceptions of student nonverbal classroom behavior. *College Teaching, 65*(1), 1–8. https://doi.org/10.1080/87567555.2016.1189390

Hoy, W. K., & Tschannen-Moran, M. (1999, May). Five facts of trust: An empirical confirmation in urban elementary. *Journal of School Leadership, 9*, 184–209.

Jahnke, J. C. (1965). Primacy and recency effects in serial-position curves of immediate recall. *Journal of Experimental Psychology, 70*(1), 130–132. https://doi.org/10.1037/h0022013

Kamenetz, A. (2020, March 19). Panic-gogy: Teaching online classes during the Coronavirus pandemic. NPR. https://www.npr.org/2020/03/19/817885991/panic-gogy-teaching-online-classes-during-thecoronavirus-pandemic.

Krathwohl, D., Bloom, B., & Masia, B. (1964). *Taxonomy of educational objectives: Affective domain.* David McKay.

Maxwell, J. (2010). *Everyone communicates, few connect: What the most effective people do differently.* Thomas Nelson.

Muller, C. (2001). The role of caring in the teacher-student relationship for at-risk students. *Sociological Inquiry, 71*(2), 241–255. https://doi.org/10.1111/j.1475-682x.2001.tb01110.x

Patience, A. (2008). The art of loving in the classroom: A defence of affective pedagogy. *Australian Journal of Teacher Education, 33*(2), 55–67. http://dx.doi.org/10.14221/ajte.2008v33n2.4

Reyes, M. R., Brackett, M. A., Rivers, S. E., White, M., & Salovey, P. (2012). Classroom emotional climate, student engagement, and academic achievement. *Journal of Educational Psychology, 104*(3), 700–712. https://doi.org/10.1037/a0027268

Roorda, D. L., Koomen, H. Y., Spilt, J. L. & Oort. F. J. (2011). The influence of effective teacher-student relationships on students' school engagement and achievement: A meta-analytic approach. *Review of Educational Research, 81*(4), 493–529. doi: 10.310-2/0034654311421793

Sieburg, E. (1985). Interpersonal confirmation: A paradigm for conceptualization and measurement. *United States International University.* ERIC Document No. ED 098 634/CS 500–881

Vareia-Silva, I. (2016, May 19).Can a lack of love be deadly? *The Conversation.* https://theconversation.com/can-a-lack-of-love-be-deadly-58659

Wilkins, J. (2014, Fall). Good teacher student-relationships: Perspectives of teachers in urban high schools. *American Secondary Education, 43* (1), 52–68.

Chapter 6

My American Story

Storytelling and Songwriting Projects for Social Change

Ilah Raleigh

Lin-Manuel Miranda's groundbreaking hip-hop musical, *Hamilton: An America Musical* (2015), begins with a story told through song. The character of Aaron Burr recounts the American story of the title character, rapping,

> How does a bastard, orphan, son of a whore and a
> Scotsman, dropped in the middle of a forgotten
> Spot in the Caribbean by providence, impoverished, in squalor
> Grow up to be a hero and a scholar? (Miranda et al., 2015, p. 6)

The opening words reveal Alexander Hamilton's humble origins in the Caribbean. The lyrics Miranda wrote hint at the rest of the story: Hamilton was destined to be a central figure in the historic events surrounding the American Revolutionary War and the establishment of the United States' republic (Cayton, 2002).

Miranda read Hamilton's story as a familiar tale of migration from the Caribbean to New York City in search of a better life (Mayora, 2018). Miranda saw a theme in Hamilton's story of people achieving success through their lyrical abilities, a theme shared with many successful hip-hop artists like Jay Z and Cardi B (Miranda, 2009).

The hip-hop musical combined two inspirations: Caribbean migration and hip-hop lyricism. *Hamilton: An American Musical* (Miranda et al., 2015) inspired the design of an innovative curriculum described in this chapter. The "My American Story" project engages college students in storytelling and songwriting to facilitate their learning and development in (1) identity formation, (2) community building, and (3) social activism.

MY AMERICAN STORY: AN INTERDISCIPLINARY CURRICULUM

Students' semester-long, interdisciplinary exploration of music and cultures culminates in a project called "My American Story." This summative assessment asks students to combine storytelling and songwriting in service to their American story. To complete this project, students draw from the performing arts, songwriting, media arts, academic writing, and creative writing to produce their American story.

During the learning process, students craft lyrics and instrumental tracks, write an artist statement, share a video presentation of their work, and receive feedback based on peers' critique of their work. See figure 6.1.

In this course, students engage with music and culture in myriad ways. They experience, analyze, and collaborate on musical creation and performance. The curriculum involves the study of diverse artists, genres, and creative works. Students experiment with speaking their truths and advocating for the common good through the arts. The 15-week course prepares students to complete the "My American Story" project with ease and confidence.

Figure 6.1. My American Story Project and Multiple Artistic Disciplines.
Source: Created by Jessica Jo Noonan.

Students use the concept of "musicking," defined as any time we participate in music making (Small, 1998), to study how they use music in their daily lives. Delving into the concepts of presentational and participatory music making (Turino, 2008), students study music in diverse contexts, cultures, and eras.

Lessons in songwriting and digital music production and explorations of music-related concepts through experiential learning support student development throughout the course. At the end of each module, students forgo papers and exams, and instead design projects to share and critique with their peers. Modules typically focus on more than one course objective, helping students increase their mastery of the course objectives using a "scaffolding" approach.

Course Objectives

The course's curriculum design is guided by seven objectives, which ask students to

1. examine and reflect on their identity and the role of musicking in their life;
2. *musick* by actively listening to, performing, and creating music;
3. guide and participate in shared community musicking experiences;
4. examine and challenge White supremacy ideology in American music education, music making, and the music industry;
5. explore social justice issues and use the arts to advocate for the common good;
6. question, critique, and share their perspectives on musicking and social justice issues; and
7. use their creative expression to build community, define and assert their identity, and influence fellow community members.

Students demonstrate their completion of the objectives listed above with their final project, "My American Story." The following sections explain how the course prepares students to create art, even when they do not conceive of themselves as artists.

The "My American Story": An Interdisciplinary Project

Students' semester-long exploration of music and culture culminates in a project called "My American Story." This final project asks students to combine storytelling and songwriting in service to their American story. Students (1) craft lyrics and instrumental tracks; (2) write an artist statement; (3) share a video presentation of their work; and (4) receive feedback based on peers' critique of their work.

The 15-week course prepares students to complete the final project (and assessment) with ease and confidence. Few students enrolled in this course have an interest in pursuing a music-related major or career pathway. Most start the semester with an identity tied to music consumption, rather than music creation or performance. The "My American Story" project can be challenging, especially to students who do not already consider themselves artists or lack training in music performance, songwriting, or digital music production.

Fortunately, most students begin the course with at least a year or two of experience in a K–12 school band or choir. They typically have some background making music using a digital audio workstation (DAW). Contemporary composers create songs using DAW software programs. DAW software provides the tools needed to compose and produce digital music with sound samples, synthesizers, and recorded sounds (LANDR, 2022). Songwriters and other composers combine and edit these various types of audios to create contemporary songs (LANDR, 2022).

Many students are familiar with the DAW Garage Band as Apple preinstalls the program on its smartphones, tablets, and computers (Apple, 2022). Still, creating a song from scratch can be challenging. Anatole, for example, shared how he "wanted . . . to complete this creative expression without any help. I was on [BandLab] for hours trying to match the melodies of the lyrics to the instrumental." To learn the songwriting skills necessary for the "My American Story" project, students learn to use BandLab, a free, cloud-based DAW, which allows musicians to collaborate remotely on joint projects (BandLab, 2022).

In recent years, students are often exposed through the Internet and social media to international music genres. Many students enter this course as committed fans of Korean K-Pop and Afrobeats. Students typically have a deep awareness of current artists, songs, and trends in contemporary commercial music (CCM). They possess knowledge, sometimes even expertise, in instrumentation, musical repertoire, genres, styles, and dance and music performance practices from multiple cultures.

However, despite many students' wealth of prior musical experiences and knowledge, students with limited music-making experience do not typically identify as artists and may doubt the arts can enrich their lives. The arts may seem a frivolous distraction from their primary goal—graduation and entry into their career pathway.

Students are often surprised to discover at the end of the course that they have artistic talent and ability. Through hard work, they develop artistic skills that they can use to express themselves in poetry, music, or performance long after the course has ended. They also acquired critical thinking skills, which are of use in fields outside of the arts. Finally, students learn about themselves through their creative work in this course.

One student, Anatole, described the difficulty and rewards of this project: "Making this song was probably one of the hardest assignments because it made you think deeper than I really would. It would make me ask why for a lot of things I do." Many of Anatole's peers echoed his sentiments. Students' journey from music consumer to music creator is outlined in the next section on course modules.

COURSE MODULES

Organized into five modules, this course helps students develop and apply the knowledge and skills needed to become storytellers and songwriters in their American Story. The concepts found in the course modules guide the course design, and students' learning throughout the semester.

Module 1 introduces the musical theories of Small (1998) and Turino (2008). Students reflect on the role and purpose of music in their daily lives, as well as their personal musical context and musical identity. In an early assignment, students share songs that represent music their families and friends exposed them to, music that makes them feel most like themselves, and music that represents an important time, person, or event in their life. Finally, they share their personal theme song or a song that speaks to their experience in the present moment.

Building on this foundation of students' personal connections to music, the course guides students in an exploration of music in a variety of social contexts and applications. Over the course of modules 2 through 5, students study artists, musical genres, musical works, and current issues in contemporary music and music education. All modules, except for the first one, end with a demonstration of their learning through creative expression.

The focus of module 2 involves the study of two mid-20th-century divas: Umm Kulthum, Egyptian star of classical Arabic song, and Maria Callas, celebrated Greek-American opera star. Students compare the careers of these powerful performers and analyze the lasting impact on their respective genres and audiences. Discussions explore the ways in which gender roles, social expectations, and sexism influence an artist's contributions to culture and their connection with the audience. The module assessment asks students to identify their personal power and represent it using an artistic medium and discipline of their choosing.

In module 3, students study the influence of African diasporic cultures on traditional and contemporary commercial musical styles throughout the

Americas and Caribbean. Students embark on a sonic journey and trace a specific rhythmic pattern, the *clave*, through the music samples drawn from countries and cultures over the space of more than two centuries.

Students develop a greater understanding of the African cultural retentions, which influenced most of the music they listen to today. They engage in cultural criticism and debate questions of cultural appropriation, cultural appreciation, and cultural sharing. Students reflect on historical forces, like the transatlantic slave trade, wars, or the murder of George Floyd and the subsequent uprising, which impacted their families. They represent the forces, aesthetics, and traditions that shaped their identity in their second creative expression.

Students turn from personal exploration to a critique of White supremacy in education for module 4. They study how White culture is often the hidden norm in music education—both in K–12 and higher education. They reflect on how their education may have served them, and, at times, harmed them. As part of their creative expression, students imagine a new music education canon and curate a sample playlist of ten essential songs every 21st-century American child should learn in school.

Module 4 guides students in a reassessment of their education and their own abilities using critical thinking skills. Student awareness of these skills and their use provides a "value-added" benefit of this class. The final module, module 5, opens with a study of Lin-Manuel Miranda's *Hamilton: An American Musical* (Miranda et al., 2015) and ends with the "My American Story" final project, which is a culmination of the three scaffolding assignment series. Students follow a discovery process and use critical thinking skills to create their American story.

Developing critical thinking skills benefits students and prepares them for their future education and profession, and/or participation in their communities as members of the greater society. We need young adults who can examine complex, real-world problems, and social issues, such as climate change or political instability, and confidently state, "I can imagine a creative solution to this problem!"

This course offers lessons in solidarity, musical advocacy, and activism—lessons which are immediately applicable to students' daily lives. These lessons are especially valuable to marginalized students reaching adulthood in turbulent times. The use of culturally sustaining pedagogy (Alim & Paris, 2017) ensures marginalized students feel included and supported in a safe learning environment.

Culturally Sustaining Pedagogy

The vital element supporting student success involves a targeted, anti-racist curriculum. Culturally sustaining pedagogy (CSP; Alim & Paris, 2017) celebrates the identities and cultural backgrounds of traditionally marginalized students, viewing students' identities and cultures as assets instrumental to their success. CSP supports students' acquisition of the knowledge, skills, and tools necessary to succeed in academia (Alim & Paris, 2017).

CSP affirms that "[educational] equity and access can best be achieved by centering the dynamic practices and selves of students and communities of color in a critical, additive, and expansive vision of schooling" (Alim & Paris, 2017, p. 3). This pedagogy encourages educators to move beyond the traditional Western European canon and to create curriculum founded on the students' strengths, abilities, and knowledge.

CSP does not ask traditionally underrepresented students to assimilate or acculturate to mainstream White American culture. Educators work with students and their communities to sustain the languages, cultural practices, and abilities to nourish and foster students' growth (Alim & Paris, 2017). The learning environment favors a collaborative learning community of empowered students and nurturing instructors. Educators encourage students to critique both the dominant culture and their own culture of origin to discover what best serves them (Alim & Paris, 2017).

Lack of awareness of a pro-White bias can lead students racialized as non-White to discount their own knowledge, experience, and identity. A guided examination of the hidden tendencies and agendas behind the cultural influences in their lives awakens students' understanding of their positionality and agency. The adoption and use of the principles and characteristics of CSP are evident in the music and cultures introduced in this course. Critical thinking skills support the processes and strategies needed in the creative process.

CRITICAL AND CREATIVE THINKING SKILLS

The course piques the interest of non-artists and ensures their engagement because of the invitation to learn. Students create music and develop skills in varied artistic disciplines. One successful engagement tactic is to stress the unexpected benefits of an artistic practice, such as developing critical thinking skills.

Students practice critical thinking skills when composing a song or writing song lyrics. They reflect on the assignment prompt and determine a vision for what they want to say and how they want to communicate it to their audience. Students use various figures of speech and forms of storytelling like metaphor, simile, symbolism, analogy, and parable to creatively communicate their story or message.

Invariably, students encounter challenges they must address to complete their creative assignments. Students reflect on the challenge, analyze it, and develop innovative, creative solutions to resolve it. Once the work is completed, students critique or analyze their peers' work and communicate their findings with respect and honesty.

In these various ways, students flex and develop their critical thinking skills during each step of their artistic practice. Strong abilities in analysis, communication, creativity, reflection, problem solving, vision, and innovation benefit all students. For example, students will find the skills of analysis, reflection, problem solving, and communication useful if they study nursing, pre-law, or education.

Creativity, vision, and innovation are useful in the fields of engineering, entrepreneurship, or digital media arts. One important concept associated with involving everyone in music participation is the idea of "musicking" (Small, 1998) described in the next section.

MUSICKING

Musicologist Christopher Small (1998) believed we need to stop thinking of music as an object, something you can buy or sell. There are many cultures for which music is something you do, often *with* other people. To signify this change to the conceptualization of music, Small (1998) invented the term *"musicking,"* [meaning] *"to take part, in any capacity, in a musical performance, whether by performing, by listening, by rehearsing or practicing, by providing material for performance (what is called composing), or by dancing"* (emphasis in original, Small, 1998, p. 9).

Musicking (Small, 1998) demythologizes music making. The music classroom becomes a safe, democratic space where all students are equal, and all efforts are welcome. Over the course of the semester, students explore the concept of musicking and study musicking in cultures. Each student considers musicking in their life, shares how they musick in class, and learns to musick like their peers.

In preparation for these shared musicking experiences, students read musicologist Thomas Turino's (2008) intriguing theories on identity and music performance, both live and recorded. These dynamic concepts are explored in the next section.

PRESENTATION AND PARTICIPATORY MUSIC

Drawing on his study of diverse music cultures, Turino (2008) defined "four musical fields" (p. 26), which include two "live performance" (p. 90) fields: "presentational and participatory" (p. 26) and two "recording music" (p. 91) fields: "high fidelity and studio audio art" (p. 67). The first two performance fields are the focus of the course.

Music making in the presentational field is specialized, competitive, and stressful (Turino, 2008) due to the expectations held for musicians and their professional work. Turino (2008) described the expectations and standards of the "presentational" field:

- music is commodified; presentational performers sell it as they perform for an audience;
- all presentational musicians are held to the same professional standard, whether they are professionals or amateurs;
- performers are valued and ranked according to their unique qualities and individual abilities; and
- musicians are the center of attention, while the audience quietly, even silently, observes the special few on stage.

Students in the course typically identify the music they experienced in K–12 schooling as presentational.

In participatory music there is no distinction between performers and audience (Turino, 2008). Everyone is making music together (Turino, 2008). More important than whether music is marketable is how the music makes the hybrid audience-performers feel (Turino, 2008). Participatory music fulfills the need for shared musical and emotional experiences that define a common group identity (Turino, 2008). Students recognize the music they make with friends and family, typically in informal settings, as participatory. The "My American Story" project engages both the presentational and participatory modes.

Through the arts, people integrate, or explore and then blend, the various parts of their individual identities into a cohesive whole (Bateson as cited in Turino, 2008). Collective performance of music supports the development of a collective spirit, which can then be used to achieve collective goals, such as fighting for social change (Turino, 2008). Students develop an artistic practice by engaging in the creative practice.

BUILDING CORE COMPETENCIES IN SONGWRITING AND STORYTELLING

Artistic Practice 101

Artists create through a four-stage process. Artists first observe the world and draw from their observations to find ideas. They allow their curiosity and passion to guide them in studying and learning more about specific topics. They reflect deeply on what they have experienced and learned. They creatively record their observations, learning, and reflections. Finally, the artist responds to the world by creating a new work.

Students rehearse this process through "Creative Notes," a group activity that mimics the creative process of *observe—learn—reflect—create*. These assignments ask students to outline the main ideas of two anchor texts by Small (1998) and Turino (2008) and convert mental concepts into artistic representations. Students continue to develop this skill as they adopt a regular artistic practice.

Students maintain a notebook of running commentary on course content, recording what they find most compelling about the readings, music, and films they encounter and their responses to their experiences.

This manner of notetaking allows for student-directed learning, which aligns with how artists learn. Students experiment with unusual note-taking methods, such as mind maps or song and video playlists. Later, when it's time to create the end-of-module creative expressions, students reflect on the past observations and learning recorded in their notes until they feel the stirrings of inspiration.

Scaffolding Assignments

Using extensive scaffolding of assignments, students gradually learn and acquire the skills and habits of working artists—each lesson and/or strategy builds and extends previous knowledge. At each stage of the scaffolding process, students depend less on the teacher and rely more on their own vision and artistic spark. Their confidence and sense of independence steadily grows. Ultimately, even the most reluctant or insecure scholar embraces their innate artistry.

Three types of scaffolded assignments, listening journals, songwriting lessons, and end-of-unit creative projects, are explained in the following section.

Listening Journals Series

Students complete an individual, low stakes listening journal at the start of each module. After selecting a track from a video playlist and listening to it multiple times, students complete a creative writing journal in response to a prompt. The instructor-curated playlists introduce the content focus of the module. Over the course of five journals, students explore narrative and descriptive writing styles: memoir, essay, poetry, short story, letter, and song lyrics. Students share the final product directly with the instructor. This series develops the skill of lyric writing for the final project.

Songwriting Series

Over the course of ten low-stakes lessons, students collaborate on a songwriting project. Students acquire digital music production skills using the free digital audio workstation (DAW) BandLab. Student groups, or "teams," create two songs while studying the basic building blocks of songwriting and music production. Students learn about melody, harmony, rhythm, genre, song structure, loops, and editing. In the final lesson, students experiment individually with free writing, or creative writing brainstorming, to develop lyrics for their final course project.

Each semester some Muslim students share that they consider performing or creating music *haram*, or "forbidden by Islamic law" (Merriam-Webster, "Haram," 2022). In these instances, Muslim students co-create alternative assignments with the instructor, such as becoming the project manager and resident coach for the team project. They evaluate each members contributions, make suggestions, and offer encouragement.

At the end of the semester, students apply the knowledge and skills acquired in these group lesson activities to create an individual song for the final course project: "My American Story." The following section outlines the third assignment series, which prepare students for the final project.

End-of-Unit Creative Projects

The end-of-module creative projects consists of a creative expression and an artist statement. The artist statement serves as a bridge between the creative work and the audience, sharing how the creative work responds to the prompt and explaining the artist's inspiration and vision for their work. Students present their high-stakes assignment in class. A peer completes a written critique for each artist. During the in-class sharing, students complete a four-step critiquing process: describe, analyze, interpret, and evaluate. Participation in this critique allows students to understand and appreciate intellectual and cultural activity.

This project and summative assessment allowed students to demonstrate their individual learning and achievement of course objectives in the last module. The creative expression involves an original work in the student's preferred discipline and artistic medium. Students may produce a creative writing piece or sculpture, record an original dance piece or musical work, or use media arts to create a visual work. Students may mix media or explore ideas outside of these suggestions. The next section introduces the inspirations and influences behind the final project, its organization, students' experiences, and examples drawn from student work.

THE FINAL PROJECT: EXAMPLES OF STUDENT WORK

This section features samples of work from 11 students who successfully completed "American Story" projects in Fall 2021. Students agreed to share samples of their songs, lyrics, artist statements, and critiques of their peer's projects and I adopted pseudonyms to disguise the identity of 11 students (approved by the Institutional Review Board, 2022). The samples and descriptions of student work provide examples of the content, process, product, and effect of differentiation in this course.

My American Story Project: Structure

The final project involves the creation of an original solo song with a digitally recorded instrumental track and sung and/or spoken vocals based on the student's selected narrative. Students create a video presentation of their song and artist statement and share it on an online forum. Each student is assigned a peer's project to formally critique.

The "My American Story" project asks students to engage in multiple artistic disciplines. Students explore

- creative writing as they craft song lyrics;
- academic writing for the drafting of the artist statement;
- songwriting as they compose instrumental and vocal tracks;
- the performing arts when they play instruments, sing, rap, or perform spoken word;
- music production with the recording of their songs using a digital audio workstation (DAW); and
- video production for the recording of the project presentations.

Selecting a Story

Like Lin-Manuel Miranda, students tell an original American story in song. This multistep project serves as the summative assessment for the course. To complete the assessment, students first reflect on the hybrid identities that they and their family and friends formed in response to transculturation and assimilation. Next, students examine and reflect on the role of musicking in their lives and identify an American story they feel must be shared. Finally, students tell this story in song.

Students are free to select almost any subject for their story. Their story can be about an individual or a group. The person or people can be alive or dead, famous or private citizens, a stranger to them, or someone they are close to. The 11 featured students wrote about their personal stories as first-generation immigrants, inspiring stories of Americans leaders, and stories that drew on the life experiences of a close friend or family member.

Jonah and Kiki explored the immigration experiences of their respective families. Kiki shared, "In Mexico, people are encouraged to immigrate to the U.S. . . . They say that you can get a good job right away and be paid well . . . within no time, you can come back to Mexico and help your family out of poverty. That is what we call the 'American Dream.'" Jonah shared his realization that "in a way my American story isn't mine at all, it's a manifestation of my parent's endurance and resilience to get me and my family here based on the fact of wanting to achieve a better life."

Like Lin-Manuel Miranda, Farrah, Charles, and Henri told stories about trailblazing Americans. Farrah told a tale that intertwined Bessie Coleman's and Amelia Earhart's individual "journey as revolutionary aviators/pilots." Charles told the story of NASA mathematician Katherine Johnson, whose life "shows that the multifaceted nature of the American Story is dependent not only on who are, but also what you look like, and what you represent for others." Henri wrote about civil rights icon Malcolm X and "his transformation of the revolutionary man he would become."

Isabelle and Edson followed a different track and told a story close to home. Isabelle's best friend inspired her to celebrate the friend's "persistence, hard-work, creativity, positivity, ambition, and pursuit of happiness." Edson, meanwhile, told the story of his grandfather, an immigrant from Europe: "This story of struggle, hard work, and perseverance inspired me to write the song about honoring his life."

The story selection process engages students' interest. Students employ the critical thinking skills of reflection to select a story, analysis to determine how to fit the story into a song lyric format, communication to tell the story, and creativity to interpret and dramatize it. Once their stories are selected, students execute the music and lyrics.

Multiple students remarked on the self-knowledge they acquired through the storytelling process. Students develop new insights into themselves and their lives as they engage in the process of crafting their stories and setting them to song. Students also gain fresh perspectives on their life through listening to their completed songs at the end of the course. Their peers provide them with valuable feedback on their finished projects, which also supports them in seeing themselves in new ways.

Composing a Song

Students have free rein as they compose their songs. Each student must determine the characteristics of the instrumental and vocal tracks, the song structure, and the lyrics. Students consider their options and develop the instrumental track, song track, and write the lyrics. Students frequently turn to an artist, a group, a song, an album, or a genre as sources of musical inspiration. Delphine, for example, wrote that she "leaned on other famous artists, such as Jessie Reyez and Sam Smith to listen to the sounds they used."

Other students look for non-musical inspiration, especially for the lyrics: nature, books, art, architecture, and the news. The protagonists of Farrah's story influenced the sound she created for her song. She wrote, "Both of them [Bessie Coleman and Amelia Earhart] being pilots/aviators also inspired the voice effect I used because it reminded me of what it sounds like when pilots communicate over radios. Finally, both women inspired the music because there is a plane-like sound in the beat to represent the planes they flew."

Students are often surprised to learn how difficult it can be to write song lyrics, especially for the chorus. While they can give free rein to their storytelling impulses in the verses, students must be more constrained for the chorus. First, students reflect and analyze the verses to discover one or two main themes. They then must use their creativity to distill the often-complex theme(s) into a few short lines. Three students, Farrah, Henri, and Delphine elegantly summarized the main themes of their songs in the chorus lyrics.

Farrah's chorus gave voice to Bessie Coleman and Amelia Earhart, "Flying through the sky / We were up so high / We were the first ones to do it / Until we left without a goodbye." This chorus about the two women aviators addresses three main themes: "both were pilots, the first . . . women . . . [in] the industry, [and] had flying related deaths." Farrah's writing, vocal timbre, and the sound effects effectively conveyed a spirit of adventure and a sense of loss.

Henri's song also portrayed the fictional thoughts of a historic figure. In his chorus, the character of Malcolm X sang, "But I'll prove them wrong / Become a revolutionary / Go to the haj [sic] / Change the world / And I'll prove them wrong / Prove them wrong / Prove them wrong." Henri wrote that examining the life of Malcolm X allowed him to address "the question of whether or not people can change, despite having a horrible past."

Finally, Delphine beautifully expressed her struggles as a multicultural Mexican American woman finding a balance between her two cultures. Her song's chorus included the words "My American story / Two cultures in one / Neither one nor' thee other / Rather my own way and under my control." Whether speaking for someone else or themselves, Farrah, Delphine, and Henri touched on common themes shared by many marginalized people in the U.S.

Isabelle sought inspiration for the song about her best friend: "listening to musicians and genres we both like, which inspired me to begin writing the music first. Some musicians I listened to were chevy, mxmtoon, cavetown, and Rebecca Sugar, which cover pop, alternative, indie, and ballad genres. Common themes I found were those of comfort, hope, and remembrance." These influences helped Isabelle write a sprightly song featuring her vocals and ukulele in tribute to her friend.

A heartbeat inspired Jonah's music and lyrics. His song begins with two chords in a rising progression played on a synthesizer. We hear their voice saying, "In the belly, I could hear my mother's heartbeat" and then the quintessential staggered rhythm of two heartbeats: THUMP-thump, THUMP-thump. They explained: "From the stories I've heard of my parent's journey, one thing that always happens to me is that my heartbeat increases . . . from the beat to the lyricism I incorporate the significance of a heartbeat throughout the piece . . . the heart is such a vital part of who we are, and I wanted that to be a significant part of my song."

Kiki combined American and Mexican musical influences to create her instrumental track: "I start off with melodies that would sound typical in an American pop/emotional song." She added Latin American elements like "maracas and then a guitar playing in a cumbia style. Both sounds which are typically found in most Mexican music, and I picked cumbia because of the popular dance in Latin America." Finally, she sampled Guillermo del Toro's Hollywood Walk of Fame acceptance speech because "he had addressed the fact that he's Mexican and that despite the struggles we face, to keep pushing and work hard."

Students craft lyrics using writing techniques introduced in earlier assignments, such as short poems, micro short stories, and three-minute free writing sessions on a variety of predetermined topics. Some students turn to story, poetry, and song forms from their cultural background, or mimic the style of a particular songwriter or rapper.

After a semester of collaboratively composing songs, students often turn to their classmates for feedback and support. Anatole shared that he asked a cohort mate for help and found that "asking him helped me solve those problems easier and much quicker [than] if I didn't seek help." At times, students seek out the instructor to brainstorm solutions to creative problems or to work past writer's block.

Each semester students rise to the challenge of creating an artistic work that demonstrates the summation of their learning and achievement of course objectives. They respect the rule that all songs must feature original melodies and lyrics. Students reflect deeply, share with honesty, and stand in their truth to express their perspective and experience in song.

Song lyrics and composition are additional tasks that engage students in multiple forms of critical thinking. Students must reflect and analyze their stories to creatively communicate through lyrics. Writing succinct song lyrics requires problem solving and innovation to stay true to both one's vision and a rhyme scheme. Students employ their creativity, communication skills, and innovation as they select instruments, create beats, and record elements for the songs. They must continually analyze sound and reflect on the feel or mood they are creating.

Any brief sample of prerecorded audio or chord progressions borrowed from other songs is altered significantly and used as only a starting point for their work. Edson, for example, repurposed the chord progression from a popular contemporary song for his song. He wrote, "I used a website to borrow the cords [sic] from Billie Eilish's song on this occasion. I used the chords, modified them, and applied them for my chorus." Edson and his peers attributed all borrowed elements in the artist statement, as required.

Writing an Artist Statement

Students discuss their work, creation process, and inspiration in a three-to-four-page artist statement. They explain how their story is an American story, how the story inspired the song, and they describe their songwriting process. They review the critical thinking skills they employed to complete each element in the final project. Students assert how their final project is a summation of their learning and builds on the exploration and engagement they demonstrated on earlier assignments.

Presenting the Work

Upon completion of the song and artist statement, the three cohorts join for a final sharing. By this stage in the semester, students are ready for this rite of passage. No longer shy or unsure, they claim the truth expressed in their creative work before friends and strangers.

Students present their story, the content of their artist statement, and their original song in an engaging five- to ten-minute presentation. Most students present their work in a fun, innovative, and creative manner. Students share attributions for any artistic or scholarly work that they quote or share during the presentation. This includes video clips, music, or images by other artists.

All artists confront insecurities, no matter their age or experience. These insecurities may manifest as apologies or disclaimers before sharing their work. It is common to hear an artist tell the audience, "It's still a work in progress," or "My voice was super hoarse," or "This probably sounds silly, but." In preparation for sharing, students and the instructor discuss a fledgling artist's tendency to hide or obscure their brilliance.

Throughout the semester, students grapple with the impulse to rush ahead and disparage their work or artistry before an audience can. By the final presentation, students typically arrive at a place of self-acceptance and even pride. They share their work without disclaimers and do not allow their fear to hold them back.

Brave Sharing and Compassionate Critique

The instructor assigns each student a peer's work to critique. After watching the peer present, students describe, analyze, and interpret the final creative expression of their peer in their own words. The reviewer describes the shared story, how it illustrates an American story, and the ways in which the artist-scholar incorporates musicking. The reviewer is asked to analyze how the work is, or is not, successful in achieving the artist's stated goals. Finally, the reviewer compares their colleague's project to their own.

This final critique asks students to actively engage with another student's creative work. Each reviewer demonstrates an understanding and appreciation of an intellectual and cultural activity.

Additional Project Samples

Anatole's American story drew on lessons from his life: rising above adversity, his sustaining relationship with his mother, learning through loss, and "understanding my purpose." These themes were encapsulated in his song's chorus:

> *Tryna find a way to get it*
> *Momma stressed out I'm the one she count on*
> *She went through a lot I won't forget it*
> *Missing all my family and friends that's long gone*
> *Helping me through life I won't regret it*
> *Blessed to be 20 with no worries I'm all grown*
> *Could've been worse if I admit it.*

Anatole's song features a simple instrumental track of a trilling instrument playing over keyboard chords. The spoken vocals are pitched but not sung. He delivers the lyrics with a somber, sober tone, which conveys strength, maturity, and reflection. Together, these elements cast a confessional quality over the song, like someone speaking to themself.

Beatrice's story uses hair as a metaphor for the African American experience. She grew up in a majority-Black neighborhood, where everyone looked like her, and she bonded with her friends over their hair texture.

> *Our coiled hair signified that we came from the same background*
> *Also the same struggle that we had in general.*
> *Not the struggle to maintain it,*
> *But the struggle of the misinterpretation of it.*

Later, when she changed schools as an older child, she was surrounded by White children:

> *Their hair was blond, brunette, and red;*
> *Mine was not.*
> *Their hair was straight, as if you could run a comb right through it;*
> *Mine was not.*
> *I felt lost.*

This new environment confused her at first and she struggled to love her hair. Beatrice has since grown to love her hair and appreciate its unique, defining qualities.

Gigi created an evocative song featuring philosophical ruminations about race spoken with a rhyming, lilting rhythm. Over atmospheric, suspended synthesizer chords and overlaid by isolated keyboard notes, the listener appears to float as they listen to a young woman speak with simplicity and wisdom:

> *Race should be erased.*
> *We question who we should praise.*
> *The truth is we are all the same.*
> *We categorize by race,*
> *But we should be ashamed.*

The song ends with Gigi's final verdict and call to action:

> *We are human.*
> *We are one.*
> *We should do something*
> *To get this mess undone.*

Race is not something we should care about.
Race is something we can live without.

The song's stark simplicity speaks straight to the heart.

Charles's song about Katherine Johnson and "the contradictory nature of the 'American Dream'" was one of the more musically advanced tracks that semester. The introduction featured a collection of wild and wonderful sounds possibly inspired by electronic dance music (EDM).

First, we hear a guitar strumming, then deep-toned, percussive synthesizers. The instrumental track changes to more a symphonic, movie soundtrack feel. Random sounds begin to encroach, layering over the synthesizer chords until suddenly the sound transforms again, recreating an early 1980s hip-hop song with Roland TR 808 drum samples. The percussion elements continue throughout, with timpani, Jamaican steel drums, and twinkling star sounds. All these changes undergird the shifting moods of the text.

Charles delivered the song's lyrics with a mix of speeds—sometimes slow and deliberate as if lecturing on a podcast, and other times fast and staccato, rapid-fire rapping. The best example of this type of delivery is used for the following thirteen lines of text delivered in a mere 27 seconds:

> *Her story isn't just a tale of easygoing success,*
> *So don't just chalk it up, to some trials and tribulations, like the rest,*
> *cuz she sparked their souls with her boundless curiosity,*
> *she was luminosity that lit with true fiery-osity,*
> *A force to be reckoned with not taken comically,*
> *kept focus methodically,*
> *who knows, how hard she had work to shine with such brilliance,*
> *it took true resilience,*
> *hand solving problems that gave computers new levels of resistance,*
> *wasn't withered by the chronically idiotic crass upper brass*
> *even then she still put them to shame*
> *guess that's why NASA couldn't put out her flame,*
> *it's no wonder you'll end up remembering Katherine's name*

It is necessary to listen to this exciting song multiple times to capture all the brilliance of the text.

SUMMARY

The "My American Story" project and summative assessment design allows for differentiation in response to students' diversity of cultural backgrounds, musical interests, educational needs, and academic abilities. This pedagogy builds on Tomlinson's (2001) work on differentiated instruction: "the teacher proactively plans and carries out varied approaches to content, process, and product in anticipation of and response to student difference in readiness, interest, and learning needs" (p. 7). The educational benefits of the project are achieved through differentiation of course content, course and assignment process, and assignment products.

Students enjoy the freedom to design a personalized version of the final project, which effectively demonstrates the individual learning they achieved. While the exact population of this school is unique, diversity is increasingly common in university classrooms. This inclusive and culturally sustaining "arts" pedagogy (Alim & Paris, 2017) may be of use to educators working with student populations that are similarly diverse in terms of race and ethnicity, religion, language, and/or previous academic experience and abilities.

Over the course of a semester, first-generation college students in a music and culture course embrace their inner artist. They observe the world and learn, reflect, and create as artists do. They develop an artistic practice, while examining their beliefs about music and music making. Students learn about music through creation and collaboration with their peers. They actively describe, analyze, interpret, and evaluate their peers' artistic work. They develop critical and creative thinking skills in new and unexpected ways. For the summative assessment, "My American Story," students design a multipart project that tells their American story through song.

The story, lyrical content, and impact of Lin-Manuel Miranda's musical theater work *Hamilton: An American Musical* (Miranda et al., 2015) inspired the design of the "My American Story" project. Lin-Manuel Miranda expanded the American Musical canon with his work on the forgotten early American. Miranda recontextualized symbols associated with the White American experience and White interpretation of American History (Mayora, 2018). Miranda leveraged the power of hip-hop to speak on the contemporary immigrant experience in America. In *Hamilton*, Miranda tells an American story that is larger than the life of Hamilton.

Many students have already experienced racism, xenophobia, misogyny, Islamophobia, classism, homophobia, and/or other forms of prejudice and hatred in their young lives. To tell their American story, they articulate and integrate their individual and group identities, exploring what it means, for example, to be born in one country but become the citizen of another. These experiences are often marginalized and ignored in traditional classroom settings. Jonah voiced the perspective of many students when he wrote, "I had so much to say about my life that has never been asked of me in an academic setting."

Adulthood is the time of exploring who you are, who you will become, and how you will impact the world around you. Educators working with diverse learners have the responsibility to guide young scholars as they become contributing members of society. Armed with the knowledge and skills only the arts can provide, our future leaders can develop into flexible, creative problem solvers ready to take on the challenges of their times.

Living in a democracy, educators have a further charge to bring the next generation of young people into the civic life of our country. This duty is made more challenging given the ways in which our divisive history is embedded in our institutions. Learning about the arts and creating artistic works allows students to examine and release the burdens of the past and see beyond the imposed limitations of the present.

For students entering college today, the events, policies, and rhetoric of the past six years are the norm. As one student, Anatole, wrote, "I think that after Trumps [sic] presidency, immigrants have become demonized and dehumanized." Students came of age as the president of the United States made public statements disparaging people like them, endorsed White supremacy, and created a hostile environment in which suspicion and violence flourished.

In *Storytelling for Social Justice*, Bell (2020) described how storytelling can be used to address racism and similar injustices in U.S. society. Students created "emerging/transforming stories . . . [taking up] the mantle of antiracism and social justice work through generating new stories that catalyze contemporary action against racism" (Bell, 2020, p. 89). In our divisive times, we need opportunities, such as the "My American Story Project," to engage new generations in the process of renewing and fortifying our democracy through storytelling and the arts.

Storytelling through song is an act of social activism through self-definition. Students' understanding of who can claim an American story and an American identity is broadened and enriched through the "My American Story" summative assessment. In sharing their story, students assert their right to take part in the story-making, which is central to our democracy. They become integrated into the American community without coerced assimilation or acculturation. Each new song created in the "My American Story" project continues the process of democratic revitalization. These songs remind us, as Delphine wrote so eloquently, that "this is my story. This is an American story like any other, there isn't just one American story, but rather hundreds and millions of different perspectives."

In recent years, media figures and politicians seek to narrowly redefine who is a "real" American. Their words and actions exclude, oppress, and harm those outside of that definition. In truth, everyone in the U.S. possesses an American story: whether they were born here or more recently arrived, no matter their race, ethnicity, religion, sexual orientation, gender identity, or the myriad ways one can define oneself. In *Hamilton: An American Musical* (Miranda et al., 2015), Miranda models one possible response to this rise of White supremacy and nationalism. We can tell a new story—a transformative one.

REFERENCES

Alim, H. S., & Paris, D. (2017). What is culturally sustaining pedagogy and why does it matter? In D. Paris & H. S. Alim (Eds.), *Culturally sustaining pedagogies: Teaching and learning for justice in a changing world*, 1–21. Teachers College Press.

Apple. (2022). GarageBand for Mac. Apple.com. Retrieved March 30, 2022. https://www.apple.com/mac/garageband/

BandLab. (2022). About BandLab [Blog post]. Blog.BandLab.com. https://blog.bandlab.com/about/

Bell, L. A. (2020). *Storytelling for social justice: Connecting narrative and the arts in antiracist teaching* (2nd ed.). Routledge.

Cayton, A. (2002). Hamilton, Alexander. In *Encyclopedia of the Enlightenment*: Oxford University Press. Retrieved January 9, 2022, from https://www-oxfordreference-com.ezproxy.stthomas.edu/view/10.1093/acref/9780195104301.001.0001/acref-9780195104301-e-294

LANDR. (2022). The 10 Best DAW Apps in the World Today [Blog post]. Blog.Landr. https://blog.landr.com/best-daw/

Mayora, G. (2018, June). Rise up: Nuyorican resistance and transcultural aesthetics in *Hamilton*. *Studies in Musical Theatre*, *12*(2), 153–166. https://doi.org/10.1386/smt.12.2.153_1

Merriam-Webster. (2022). Haram. In Merriam-Webster.com dictionary. Retrieved March 31, 2022, from https://www.merriam-webster.com/dictionary/haram

Miranda, L. M. (2009, November 2). Lin-Manuel Miranda performs at the White House poetry jam: (8 of 8). The Obama White House. https://www.youtube.com/watch?v=WNFf7nMIGnE

Miranda, L.-M., Lacamoire, A., & Chernow, R. (2015). *Hamilton: An American Musical*. Hal Leonard Corp.

Small, C. (1998). *Musicking: The meanings of performing and listening*. University Press of New England.

Tomlinson, C. A. (2001). *How to differentiate instruction in mixed-ability classrooms*. Association for Supervision & Curriculum Development. ProQuest Ebook Central, https://ebookcentral.proquest.com/lib/unistthomas-ebooks/detail.action?docID=3002067.ds

Turino, T. (2008). *Music as social life: The politics of participation*. University of Chicago Press.

Chapter 7

The Centrality of Identity in the Learning Environment

Jayne Sommers and Christina Holmgren

Another racially motivated incident has taken place at the university. Jonah, a Black, nonbinary student in their second year of college, awakes to an email from the institution's president. The email states that a Black student on campus was targeted by campus police the night before. The president's email also said the institution plans to conduct an internal investigation of the incident, as well as a statement claiming this incident does not uphold the values of the campus community.

Jonah has been asked to attend a mandatory meeting with their residence hall floor to discuss the incident with their peers and resident advisor. Jonah feels wary of what may be discussed during the meeting but also anticipates an opportunity to unpack their feelings. Upon arrival at the meeting, Jonah quickly realizes they are the only Black person present. When the resident advisor asks the students in the space to share their thoughts, most students look to Jonah to begin. Feeling like they have little choice, Jonah expresses their disappointment, anxiety, and fear for their future safety on campus.

Silence fills the room after Jonah speaks until Alex, a White man, states that he believes Jonah may be overreacting. He reminds Jonah that the community does not know for sure why this Black student was approached by campus security and that until the internal investigation has been completed, they should refrain from making any judgments. Alex explains that as a gay man, he understands a fear for one's safety, but he does not believe this event rises to such concern.

Jonah leaves the meeting disheartened. Heading to their advisor's office for a scheduled appointment, Jonah hopes to discuss the emotions they have been experiencing all morning with their advisor. When Jonah enters the advisor's office, they notice she seems distracted. A White woman with an advisee load of over 200 students, she has little time to prepare for a class. The advisor teaches in an hour and does not have much time to connect with Jonah. She knows about the campus incident but has not thought much of it since reading the email from the president.

As briefly as they can, Jonah tries to put into words their experience of the meeting this morning. The advisor, still a bit distracted and seemingly overwhelmed, tells Jonah that she knows Alex and is sure that he did not intend any harm. The advisor says she knows Alex to be very engaged in social justice issues and believes that Jonah might have misinterpreted his comment. The advisor tells Jonah that they can talk more at their next appointment, but if Jonah does not have any concerns regarding their major or course scheduling, she needs to use the time to prepare for class.

With the heavy weight of invalidation on their shoulders, Jonah heads to their first class of the day. In no mood to engage with the course material and still analyzing the day's experiences, Jonah zones out, disconnected from the instructor and their student peers. The instructor, noticing Jonah's disengagement, calls on them to answer some questions. In doing so, the instructor misgenders Jonah.

****

Jonah's story illustrates the importance of centering identity in education. To center identity means to appreciate its importance and connection to all the factors affecting students' ability to engage in learning and enter classroom dialogue. Centering identity fosters a sense of belonging and a feeling of being included in authentic and meaningful ways. When professors center identity in education, they pay focused attention to the various identities presented and valued in the learning environment.

Centering identity in teaching first requires a recognition of various forms of systemic oppression. These systems have ensured the maintenance of power within particular social identity groups and the consistent marginalization of others throughout the history of the United States. Historically oppressed, marginalized, and excluded groups include Black, Indigenous, and people of color (BIPOC), women, trans* and gender nonconforming individuals, non-Christians, queer individuals, differently abled and neurodiverse people, and immigrants.

Knowledge of historically oppressed and privileged groups helps to explain why members of oppressed groups do not feel they are in the center of their educational experiences—fully seen, valued, and included. Instead, members of historically excluded groups too often reside on the margins, away from the heart of a learning environment.

Historically privileged groups include White people, men, cisgender individuals, Christians, individuals in opposite-sex partnerships, able-bodied and neurotypical individuals, and individuals born in the United States. This is not an exhaustive list of social identity groups, but it provides the foundation for our discussion. An awareness of how privilege advantages certain groups inevitably exposes and challenges the underlying assumptions of advantaged groups regarding entitlement, power, and unearned privilege.

Often, calls for critical examination of pedagogy are accompanied by data describing increased diversity of student demographics, usually with a focus on racial diversity. While these trends are indeed accurate and warrant attention by educational institutions, regardless of who sits in our classrooms, the approach to course planning and pedagogy should prioritize a recognition of the centrality of identity within all educational experiences.

No matter our discipline or area of expertise, we all teach humans who hold a variety of identities and who carry previous experiences into our classrooms. Ideally, professors and students believe in the power of educational experiences, which recognizes and honors the connections among us as humans. Honoring individual identities and fostering critical thinking about how social identities shape lives may deepen community among students and faculty.

IDENTITY IN EDUCATION

In this chapter, the term "historically excluded" signifies social identity groups for whom education was not initially intended, available, or accessible within the United States. Historically excluded includes women, Black, Indigenous, and people of color, individuals with disabilities, students from low socioeconomic backgrounds, and students from LGBTQ+ communities. This exclusion began with the conception of education in the United States.

Education's historical roots tie back to the colonization, cultural genocide, and assimilation of those who were not White, men, and Christian (Spring, 2016). Some of the earliest instances of educational methods within the United States included the kidnapping and deculturalization of Indigenous children by English colonists. Indigenous children were placed in schools specifically created to strip them of their cultural livelihood.

With the growth of the country's immigrant population, as well as the emancipation of enslaved Africans, educational systems continued to seek the cultural transformation of communities of color into European American culture and society, while also ensuring the segregation and inequitable treatment of these communities (Spring, 2016). Beyond mere exclusion, many of the most prestigious higher education institutions used the labor of enslaved

Africans to build their campuses, literally capitalizing on work performed by Black individuals (Wilder, 2013).

The United States Supreme Court ended the legalized requirement of school segregation across the country through the *Brown v. Board of Education of Topeka* decision in 1954. While this legislation was a move forward in civil rights for all communities, it did not end the cultural harm placed upon historically excluded communities, nor did it provide equal access to educational resources.

Around the same time, families of students with disabilities also fought for access to education. The Elementary and Secondary Education Act (ESEA) passed in 1965, revised in 1970, reauthorized as the Individuals with Disabilities Education Act (IDEA) in 1990, and amended in 2004, attempted to address the exclusion of students with disabilities. The new law required educational institutions from kindergarten through higher education to provide students with needed accommodations.

While these historical advances mean an increasingly diverse population may pass through the doors of our educational institutions, the exclusion of identities continues in schools and on campuses. Students navigate not only life in school and on campus, but also the reality of the broader cultural zeitgeist in which they live. Students today navigate broad realties, such as political unrest and divide, calls both for and against racial justice and debates around how to achieve it, the trauma of living through a global pandemic, proposed legislation restricting the freedoms of trans* individuals, and living in a world not designed for uniquely abled bodies, just to name a few examples. Educators have a responsibility to recognize students' lived realities are incredibly complex. The world in which students live has required many of them to mature more quickly than generations past.

Educators cannot facilitate conversations around identity and dominant power structures in meaningful ways if they have not first evaluated current cultural norms within society and education. This requires an examination of how these norms contribute, either explicitly or implicitly, to oppressive traditions and experiences for historically excluded students and community members. This chapter addresses how teachers and professors can eliminate exclusionary practices within the microsystems of their classrooms.

The "centrality of identity in education" refers to the importance of identity and its role in ensuring a truly inclusive learning environment for all students, especially those with a history of marginalization in society. Understanding the importance of identity in human experience and learning, "identity salience" explains how and why students relegated to the edges of the center feel isolated and disengage from learning (Jones & Abes, 2013). The antidote used to turn this concern around involves a change in practices and attitudes, but first, educators must develop an understanding of *why* identity is important, and how it affects not only our experiences but the meaning we make of our experiences.

IDENTITY SALIENCE

Individuals hold multiple social identities, as some of the examples in the section above suggested. Intersecting social identities not only influence what individuals experience in the world, but also shape how they make meaning of each individual experience. Holding a particular set of intersectional identities does not equate to a monolithic set of life experiences. Rather, educators need to recognize the influence of social identities on individual experiences within and outside of education.

Different social identities hold different value for individuals, depending on a variety of factors. Research on social identity often frames this concept as *identity salience* (Jones & Abes, 2013). Individuals are most likely to identify any oppressed or historically excluded identities they hold as most salient to them, particularly when they are in a space in which they perceive themselves as the only or one of few people within the group who hold a particular identity (Jones, 1997).

Additionally, *identity salience* (Jones & Abes, 2013) can be influenced by family and cultural norms, particularly in communities with strong preservation of cultural traditions. This knowledge can assist teachers to critically examine their teaching plans and learn how to more effectively center identity. Opportunities for instructors to center identity in teaching, no matter the area of focus or discipline, are described.

Educators can begin by practicing recognition of the multiplicity of identities, and appreciating the value added to educational experiences when teachers honor multiple identities and perspectives. When teachers include critical perspectives, which challenge the long-accepted foundational elements of each discipline, they may experience a true transformation in the depth and effectiveness of their teaching. The remainder of this chapter provides strategies teachers may use to center identity in their educational practice. We begin with the practice of cultural humility.

Cultural Humility

No matter how democratic or egalitarian some might aim to be in their teaching, when teachers enter the room, they unavoidably assume a position of power. Students look to teachers to guide their learning and trust that teachers will do so in ways that will enhance their lives (at least, that is the hope for many of us). As individuals who hold positional power in educational settings, it is imperative that teachers value and use continuous self-reflection and critique as the process needed to recognize the centrality of identity in educational experiences. The practice of cultural humility begins with this step.

Consider how you would answer the question "Who am I?" in the context of social identity. You may identify as a BIPOC, White, or as multiracial. You might *also* identify as straight, queer, cisgender, or nonbinary. Perhaps you also identify as a neurotypical or neurodivergent person. Think also about your physical body—when you navigate your daily life, are you "able-bodied," or do you experience a world not built for the ways your body works?

Your responses to the "Who am I?" question reflect your intersectional social identities, sometimes referred to as *positionality*. The term "intersectional" points to the fact that we never hold just *one* of our many social identities, and that our social identities influence our experiences with intersecting forms of systemic oppression (Collins & Bilge, 2020).

Individuals hold multiple intersecting identities, some of which may have been historically represented, uplifted, and empowered within education, and some of which may have been historically marginalized, excluded, and oppressed within and outside of education. Simultaneously, students holding multiple intersecting identities need a greater understanding regarding the interplay between teachers' identities and student identities.

While many instructors pride themselves in fostering dynamic learning environments, some may fail to recognize the dynamics of social identity at play and miss the opportunity to fully see, include, and engage students learning. Returning to Jonah's story, the instructor may have planned an engaging lesson, however, Jonah may have felt more excluded after entering their class.

Educators bring unconscious bias into their classrooms (requires challenging taken-for-granted assumptions), and unconscious bias may lead them to attend more to the contributions of students who share some or all their social identities. At the same time, students also enter classrooms with some level of implicit bias, which impacts the extent to which they engage with and trust those who hold differing social identities. While it is impossible to adequately address all the myriad ways intersecting social identities might influence a classroom dynamic, at the very least, teachers need to consider elements, such as assuming or building trust and the need to be transparent about their expectations of students.

The recognition of our own identities and how they might influence our effectiveness as educators can be challenging, but the rewards of practicing cultural humility certainly outweigh the costs. Given unavoidable blind spots and unconscious bias, educators can enhance their teaching by acknowledging we have much to learn from our students.

While this may sound a bit contradictory at first, this does not mean we abdicate our responsibilities as facilitators of learning or content experts. It means teachers and professors model humility about the learning edges in our work with students and acknowledge students may bring perspectives that deepen the conversation in ways teachers may not have yet identified.

Cultural humility involves listening to students who have been historically excluded when they name a lack of identification with course material and learning activities, challenge traditional thinking, or perhaps even share examples of emotional harm within the classroom.

Identifying the gifts students offer to others when they take the risk of providing constructive feedback, particularly around social identity, affirms their identities and sense of belonging. Once professors embrace cultural humility as a part of their pedagogical approach, teachers have access to a variety of additional strategies at their disposal—strategies which communicate an understanding of the centrality of identity to the learning experience.

Centering Identity in Syllabi

Even before the first day with students, teachers have opportunities to communicate their intent to center identity in their teaching. Professors and teachers demonstrate their commitment to honoring identity in accessible ways for students by sharing their teaching philosophy, designing intentional learning outcomes, embracing universal design principles, curating a collection of course materials to examine disciplines from a variety of perspectives, and creating assessments with clear criteria along with room for creativity. These strategies and actions support the necessary preparations needed before a new class or semester begins.

Sharing Your Philosophy of Teaching

Teachers must recognize the value of communicating their philosophy of teaching to students. Teachers and professors communicate the *content* of our teaching to students via the course materials and syllabi but sharing a bit about *why* and *how* we teach also has incredible value. A philosophy of teachers reveals the values that guide teaching.

A brief definition of social identities may require only a paragraph or two to explain professors' teaching philosophy, including our salient identities. The statement communicates an understanding that each of us (instructor and students included) bring a unique perspective to the classroom based on our individual identities and experiences.

This explicit naming of our understanding of social identities and our own positionality, along with a recognition of the value of students' contributions, sets the stage for engaging and rich classroom dialogue. We can also communicate a commitment to culturally sustaining pedagogy, which we discuss in detail later in this chapter.

Identity-Centered Learning Outcomes

Once students know what they can expect from their teachers and facilitators, teachers should describe what to expect regarding their own learning. Explicit and well-designed learning outcomes communicate to students the scope and focus of learning, as well as the knowledge intended for students to take with them when the class ends. As teachers who recognize the centrality of identity to the educational experience, we can audit our learning outcomes to identify opportunities for revision.

Perhaps a learning activity and outcome may require students to articulate an understanding of the course material from a variety of social identity perspectives. Or, depending on the focus of a particular course, students are expected to demonstrate an understanding of their social identities and positionality. Another example may require students to identify courses of action that interrupt existing dominant power systems. These last two types of learning outcomes may be most appropriate within higher education but may also be applicable to high school students.

Using Universal Design for Learning (UDL)

When teaching centers identity, we concern ourselves with the inclusive nature of our pedagogical approach and materials. One consideration within the concept of inclusion pertains to accessibility. Accessibility needs range from modified course material for visibly impaired students to additional exam time for students with a learning disability or chronic illness diagnosis. Increasingly, students present an infinite constellation of needs between, around, and unrelated to these examples.

Many resources are available to guide professors as they seek to ensure teaching and learning plans, activities, and resources are accessible to all students. An internet search for resources on Universal Design for Learning (or UDL) yields a plethora of materials to guide course design and practice. As the name of this approach suggests, using UDL principles enhances the educational experience for *all* students, not just some. For example, teachers and professors can ensure the headings, tables, and other content in the syllabi and other class documents are clear for all students and accessible for students using assistive technology (AT), such as a screen reader.

When using images in our course documents or teaching, we can add an "alt text" description to the image or describe it orally for students, which increases understanding of the connection between the image and the course material. Additionally, those of us who use visual platforms such as PowerPoint can learn about the importance of using contrasting colors in presentations to increase readability for all students.

Carefully Curating Course Materials

As educators who hold positional power within the classroom, one common mistake involves relying on students who hold historically excluded backgrounds to share their lived experiences to teach others about the realities of systemic oppression. Instead, educators should provide all students with a curriculum that exposes them to scholars, research, and ideologies to examine the role of power and privilege and expose systemic inequities within their disciplines.

Toward this end, teachers curate resources for students with an eye toward representation and inclusion of scholarship authored by individuals who hold a variety of social identities. At the very least, this strategy involves an audit of required materials and critical examination of contemporary scholarship within the discipline. There is an argument to include historically seminal texts, and we do not suggest abandoning their contributions altogether. However, a critical examination of the authors of these texts and the social identities they hold is in order.

Professors have an obligation to stay abreast with current scholarship authored by individuals who hold historically excluded identities, likely not represented in disciplinary works. This examination does not invite any kind of "quota" related to the social identities of source authors; rather, we simply encourage intentional inclusion of materials authored by scholars with a variety of social identities.

While representation is a vital first step, teachers have an opportunity to go even further in evolving the course content, particularly in post-secondary education. Beyond considerations of representation in scholarship, learning resources and activities may be used to introduce and evaluate conceptual and empirical scholarship commonly used in courses.

This process examines discipline through the lenses of power, privilege, and hegemonic systems to maintain the distribution of economic and political power within society. Introducing students to these critical perspectives in conversation with foundational thinking fosters critical thought, which we discuss at length later in this chapter.

Rethinking Assessments/Assignments to Include Criteria + Creativity

When designing opportunities for students to demonstrate their learning via assignments or assessments, an identity-centered approach strikes a balance between clear criteria and allowance for creativity. Students deserve to know the criteria they must meet to receive the grade they hope to earn, and rubrics provide a strong means of communicating criteria in a way students can easily understand.

Connecting course material to real life experiences allows students to employ creative means to demonstrate their knowledge. While the criteria remain the same for all students, teachers can provide options for meeting the criteria. This might involve the demonstration of learning in an essay or the submission of a piece of visual art to the creation of a video recording. When professors center identity in their teaching, they uncover more ways students might demonstrate their learning through authentic assessment. This allows students to bring themselves into their work.

PEDAGOGICAL APPROACHES TO CENTER IDENTITY

Culturally Sustaining Pedagogy

Pedagogical practice calls for educators to recognize the culturally diverse backgrounds and social identities of the students with whom they work and create educational opportunities that support these students. Culturally responsive and relevant pedagogical approaches acknowledge and affirm students' lived experiences. These approaches view the cultural wealth students bring to the classroom as an asset, and the need to ensure the inclusion of various cultures within the curriculum. New approaches to learning and the selection of resources create an inclusive educational environment for students who have been historically excluded from the curriculum and community of schools. See figure 7.1.

However, simply affirming students' existence and appreciating their culture in educational spaces is not sufficient. As educators, we must allow students to not only see a wider variety of thought within curriculum but also to recognize the structural inequities within society leading to the exclusion and oppression of these communities. A recognition of structural oppression provides students with the tools they need to enact sustainable change.

Culturally sustaining pedagogy (CSP) engages students in the work of investigating dominant societal norms through the evaluation of multiple ways of knowing. This pedagogical approach helps students to question and

Figure 7.1. Pedagogical Approaches to Center Identity.
Source: Created by Jessica Jo Noonan.

"unlearn" oppressive norms through engaging and actionable pedagogy. CSP recognizes the necessity for students to leave educational spaces with the tools to create and sustain a liberated and equitable society.

As an educational approach, CSP pulls from many critical frameworks that decenter and deconstruct harmful, and often violent, societal standards and expectations. Theoretical frameworks and methods to analyze experience, such as queer theory, crip theory, intersectionality, and critical race theory (CRT) all hold elements that show up in a classroom practicing culturally sustaining pedagogy.

The philosophical principles of queer theory place significance on disrupting heterosexual culture by evaluating discourse around sexuality and gender identity (Abes et al., 2019). The language used, texts selected, learning activities planned, and discussions facilitated may exclude or empower the identities of students or professors based on the culture and climate of the learning environment.

Discussions of identity include "what we think we know" about gender and sex, and help individuals break away from binary and categorical language contributing to the burden and oppression of members of the LGBTQ+ community. The lasting impacts of this analysis seep into societal structures that keep LGBTQ+ individuals from obtaining jobs, homes, and safety within their communities. Additionally, a culturally sustaining educational space not only includes the historical experiences of LGBTQ+ individuals within the curriculum, but also identifies how students have contributed, either explicitly or implicitly, to the harm done to these communities.

Similarly, crip theory highlights the pervasiveness of able-bodied and able-mindedness throughout societal contexts. In the same way heterosexist ideology permeates systems with beliefs of heteronormativity and assumptions on gender, ableism perpetuates and preserves the presumption of normalcy around able-bodied individuals.

These frameworks emphasize the importance of counter-narrative, storytelling, and questioning dominant viewpoints, which consist of personal experiences and membership in society. Students can learn how to leverage their positionality to dismantle inequities and promote liberatory change through guided reflection that centers students' social identities.

The pedagogical approaches fall under culturally sustaining pedagogy as an overarching framework. Each of these practices center identity, add depth to student engagement with course material, and place an emphasis on the skills needed to ensure students leave educational spaces ready to actively dismantle structures and promote liberatory practices for the common good, while also recognizing the value of self-determination and reciprocity.

Enhancing Critical Thinking

Students continually navigate an increasingly complex world where intersecting oppressions invite multi-sectional analysis. For example, the COVID-19 pandemic has shed light on racial injustices across the United States due to the profound losses experienced by communities of color at rates exceeding predominantly White communities. Increased anxiety and fear among undocumented immigrants intensified with uncertainty about the future of legislation impacting their paths to citizenship.

These realities, along with *many* more, elevate the need for students to think critically about the conditions of their communities. Before teachers engage students in conversations that challenge hegemonic ideologies, teachers must ensure their students have the necessary tools to engage in this demanding work. The ability to think critically about dominant power structures and how they maintain systemic and structural control can be an empowering experience for students in the classroom.

Thinking critically requires asking questions to interrogate assumptions and provide opportunity for counter-narratives to be heard. Teachers use various strategies to help students build their ability to think critically. Instructors provide students with the space to think deeply about any given topic by engaging them in guided conversation and participatory practices. Instructors can ask questions such as these:

- How do you know that to be true?
- What is considered "true?"
- Who benefits from this interpretation?
- Who is harmed or excluded by this perspective?
- What do your findings mean for society as a whole?

These types of questions are investigative by nature and get students in the mindset of questioning predisposed beliefs they may hold. The questions also help students recognize limitations and enhances their ability to critique existing practices, particularly around issues of systemic inequities, positionality, oppression, and power.

The role of educators in this context is to help students discover the value of inquiry. Students learn how to evaluate ideas from multiple perspectives while also recognizing how their unconscious bias may be at play in their decision making. Educators might help students do this by opening themselves up to student critique (Brookfield, 2015).

Allowing students to question why we do something in a particular way allows space for a variety of perspectives. Students are not empty vessels waiting to be filled when they arrive in our classrooms. They bring their own knowledge that can help construct the way a course is facilitated. Opening oneself up to these ideas shows students how questioning concepts can lead to innovative end results. Additionally, there may be instances when our own blind spots cause harm to students, especially those who hold backgrounds that have been historically excluded. Modeling what critical thinking looks like when questioning the assumptions that led to the harm can be a valuable opportunity in the classroom.

Contextualizing critical thinking is another strategy educators might use when developing analytical skills within students. Case studies, scenarios, and ethical dilemmas that draw upon current events and require students to investigate the role of dominant power structures help students build their skills in critical thinking. Debate teams across the United States use this practice regularly to help students evaluate topics from a variety of perspectives and understand the complexities of societal policies.

Students may find that topics that seem simple at face value (and without critical thinking) can in fact be complicated, ethically immoral, or even violent. Using real-world examples helps students identify how their own social identities or privileges contribute to their instinctual response to any given scenario. After receiving initial guidance from instructors around critical thinking strategies, students will soon make space for their own curiosities and feel empowered to ask their own questions, making for an engaging learning environment.

USING INTERGROUP DIALOGUE

Explorations of culturally sustaining pedagogical practice may cause some students to feel unsure of how to approach difficult conversations about power and privilege. The fear of saying the wrong thing, appearing apathetic or ignorant, or unintentionally causing harm to their peers can lead to high levels of anxiety among students with privileged identities.

In addition, those who hold backgrounds that have been historically excluded may also be on high alert during these conversations, worried that someone may say something that will cause them emotional harm and further contribute to feelings of isolation within the educational space. These concerns can be debilitating to the classroom culture, leading to silence and disengagement.

Practicing intergroup dialogue (IGD) in educational spaces allows students and teachers to recognize the effects of current and historical traumas and their lasting impact on historically excluded students. The practice of IGD strengthens collaboration among all students to see and dismantle oppressive systems. Intergroup dialogue relies on the recognition and accountability of systemic inequities and unearned privileges to create an educational community that fosters trust and vulnerability.

An acknowledgment of the harm caused by racism, sexism, heterosexism, ableism, and xenophobia may cause students to examine how they might use their privilege and positionality to enact structural change.

Phases of Intergroup Dialogue

Intergroup dialogue consists of four phases adopted to build a healthy classroom community, which allows potentially difficult conversations to occur. While these phases may seem linear, the nature of this dialogue means participants will likely encounter incidents in which teachers, in the role of facilitator, may need to slow down and revisit previous phases to address potential harm. These phases are meant to act as a fluid guide to help instructors understand how they might move students forward in their equity and inclusion journey.

Phase 1: Authenticity as Community Building

The honesty of naming one's anxiety around discussions of race, oppression, and privilege, particularly for those who hold positional power in these areas, is the first phase of engagement within intergroup dialogue. Themes, such as vulnerability and freedom, appear as starting points to IGD.

Participants state what they hope to gain from these conversations, their concerns about engaging in dialogue with difficult topics, and express how others hope to move forward in community and collaboration with their peers. This initial phase begins to introduce students to the idea that their fears likely arise from unconscious bias—a bias they do not know how to address. The acknowledgment that students have unconscious biases as well as their hope to recognize and understand biases to avoid causing harm to others is expressed. Educators also acknowledge their experiences with implicit or explicit bias and model how they plan to move forward in building a community with their students.

The value of this introductory phase is that it moves students away from binary thinking around what makes someone good or bad. Most hesitation around having these challenging conversations arises from the fear of not wanting to be seen as a "bad person." The belief that holding unconscious bias makes one a bad person denies the complexities of the internalization of hegemonic ideologies.

Instead, teachers can lead students in honest conversations that reveal the reality that it would be remarkable, and unheard of, for an individual raised in society to not hold unconscious bias. The authentic discussions that arise from this phase may prepare students for the more challenging work of identifying their unique relationships with systems of oppression through social identities they hold.

Phase 2: Exploration of Social Identities and Personal Connections to Systems, Power, and Oppression

One of the key components of intergroup dialogue as a pedagogical approach is its emphasis on reciprocity in both dialogue and action. Neither educators nor students should rely on those who have been historically excluded to do the work of sharing their stories and vulnerabilities in the name of student learning. This forced disclosure of microaggressions and other harmful encounters creates a culturally taxing classroom environment for this group of students and often retraumatizes them. Instead, intergroup dialogue relies on *all* students to explore their own social identities and their personal connections to systems of power and oppression.

The sharing of these stories often reveals not only differences in lived experiences, but also commonalities students share with each other. This is also when students begin to understand the complexities of intersectionality and the ability to hold both privileges and disadvantages at a structural level. Instructors cannot move into arduous conversations if students have not acknowledged their privilege and connection to systemic inequities.

Phase 3: Difficult/Courageous Conversations

Once instructors have taken the time to build trust and community through the first two phases, this third phase allows for the exploration of topics that may be seen as "hot button" topics or controversial issues in society. These topics often have direct impacts on students, and students may perceive avoidance of these topics as apathy for the student and their lived experiences.

To acknowledge a societal concern and connect it to inequitable systems allows students to recognize how power and oppression may be at play at all levels of their lives. For example, an educator may facilitate a discussion among students about affirmative action in college admissions, and why students of color, as an example, may be considered over White students within this context.

Students may discuss the history of segregation and exclusionary practices within schools at both the K–12 and post-secondary levels and the current racial demographics at four-year colleges and universities. Acting in the role of facilitator, educators might challenge students by pushing them to acknowledge the role of legacy admissions within the broader context of social capital, access, and gatekeeping within the field of college admissions.

Educators should continually connect the discussion topics back to the structural foundations upon which this country was built. This constant connection reveals this simple finding: no matter the topic, we cannot exist outside of systems of oppression, and thus, should always consider how actions can be taken to rebuild a more equitable society. Educators may also find themselves needing to pause and return to the *Exploration of Social Identities* phase while discussing hot topics, as students may fall back into unconscious biases during these conversations. This occurs when participants forget how their positionality may influence their responses.

Phase 4: Action and Sustaining Equitable Systems

It is critical that dialogue about dismantling inequitable systems leads to actionable items that students can take with them when they leave the educational space. We can ensure that students know how to translate these conversations into their everyday lives and beyond. This does not mean that students with privileged identities should leave these spaces with the intention of "saving" those from historically excluded communities.

On the contrary, those with privileged identities should recognize how they can use their positionality and privilege, in collaboration with those negatively impacted by inequitable systems, to create liberated communities. These action items might start on a smaller scale as students gain understanding of how to use their positionality, which may look like challenging friends, fellow students, or even family members in the face of unconscious bias or harmful and oppressive language.

As students develop their ability to identify their own bias and privilege through self-reflection, we can help students recognize the next steps *for them* as individuals in their journey to create and sustain equitable systems. Teachers can help students realize that each of them will be at a different level of understanding and awareness. What may seem like a small action item for one may be a necessary first step for another. Rushing students into higher-level action items before they have done the work of self-reflection and listening can have the inverse effect intended.

Incorporation of Mindfulness

The practice of a culturally sustaining pedagogical approach, with its emphasis on systemic inequities, oppression, and power, can create an experience of cognitive dissonance among some students. It is not the role of the educator to eliminate this discomfort, as these emotions are a valuable part of the learning experience and can be a sign of growth within the students. Rather, in cases like this, teachers must recognize their role as facilitators, guiding students in a way that both affirms and continues to challenge them.

An educational space is not meant to eliminate the discomfort students may experience in the face of challenging conversations around social identities and privilege. When we fail to help students interrogate their lived experience through this lens, we can inadvertently uphold oppressive traditions and practices. Instead, educators can use mindful practice techniques to help students recognize what and how they are feeling during these moments, creating space for an authentic conversation that students are better prepared to navigate.

Mindful practices in the classroom should begin with an emphasis on and understanding of the criticality of self-reflection. A mindfulness approach calls on educators to allow students time and space to assess their physical and psychological responses while engaging in these conversations (Berila, 2015). During moments of silence or visible discomfort, a teacher might pause a discussion and ask students to reflect on what is happening in their bodies: this could feel like a rush of adrenaline, elevated heart rate, fast breathing, or sweating.

We can also guide students to reflect on their mental well-being: Are they feeling defensive? Are they shutting down in response? Are they withdrawing from the conversation or dissociating? As students begin to recognize their responses, these responses become less consuming and overwhelming in the moments of dialogue. Practicing this mindful technique allows students to take note of their experiences while continuing to engage in the challenge of the conversation.

SUMMARY

The collection of strategies and pedagogical approaches described in this chapter may feel daunting to some. We may find ourselves comfortable with some of these ideas and less comfortable with others. We encourage readers of this text to identify at least one practical way to infuse social identity into their teaching.

Students, particularly those who have been historically excluded, deserve to be fully seen, represented, and heard within all educational spaces. Implementing these strategies within the classroom ensures consistent recognition of students' realities within their learning experiences. When identity is at the center of our work as educators, we can provide students with historically privileged identities the tools needed to reflect on their experiences.

The "tools" include reflecting on social identities, unearned privilege obtained due to those social identities, emotions experienced while interrogating their positionality, and using their unearned privilege to disrupt cultural norms, power structures, and belief systems, which prove oppressive and harmful to others.

As teachers move forward with a commitment to centering identity in their educational practices, we encourage reflection on the following questions:

- Does your teaching philosophy appear on your syllabus? Does it clearly communicate your commitment to honoring the centrality of identity?
- Does your course include at least one learning outcome that requires reflection on identities and the larger system of your discipline?
- Have you considered a variety of accessibility needs in the curation and creation of your course materials?
- What is the balance of identities represented in the authors of assigned readings? How might an increase in diversity in assigned readings motivate students' level of engagement and deepen their learning?

- Do the course assessments/assignments provide clear criteria for students as well as multiple options for ways students can demonstrate their learning?
- How does implicit bias impact your educational practice?
- How do your default pedagogical choices perpetuate or interrupt historical distributions of power in the classroom?
- How do you respond to instances of marginalization (from microaggressions to overt acts of oppression) in your classroom? How might you incorporate principles of mindfulness into your response?

The questions may be used to audit your current course design and learning and teaching activities to identify potential improvements to course pedagogical practices.

REFERENCES

Abes, E. S., Jones, S. R., & Stewart, D. L. (Eds.). (2019). *Rethinking college student development theory using critical frameworks*. Stylus Publishing, LLC.

Berila, B. (2015). *Integrating mindfulness into anti-oppression pedagogy: Social justice in higher education*. Routledge.

Brookfield, S. D. (2015). *The skillful teacher: On technique, trust, and responsiveness in the classroom*. John Wiley & Sons.

Collins, P. H., & Bilge, S. (2020). *Intersectionality* (2nd ed.). Wiley.

Jones, S. R. (1997). Voices of identity and difference: A qualitative exploration of the multiple dimensions of identity development in women college students. *Journal of College Student Development, 38*, 376–386.

Jones, S. R., & Abes, E. S. (2013). *Identity development of college students: Advancing frameworks for multiple dimensions of identity*. John Wiley & Sons

Spring, J. (2016). *Deculturalization and the struggle for equality: A brief history of the education of dominated cultures in the United States*. Routledge.

Wilder, C. S. (2013). *Ebony and ivy: Race, slavery, and the troubled history of America's universities*. Bloomsbury Publishing.

Chapter 8

Academic Student Procrastination
Causes and Effects on Student Learning

Sarah Noonan

Imagine a student entering an urgent care clinic for the diagnosis and treatment of a suspected case of "academic student procrastination" (AsP; Steel & Klingsieck, 2016). The waiting room is packed with other worried and exhausted students, and even a few teachers and professors. A nurse leads the patient to an examination room, asks a few questions, and hands a clipboard to the patient with questions to answer before meeting with the doctor. The questions concern a suspected case of AsP. See figure 8.1.

The answers to the questions may help doctors (or perhaps academic advisors) determine the causes, symptoms, and severity of AsP. While this imaginary visit to the urgent care clinic may seem far-fetched, the problems associated with AsP extract a real cost on students and their educational careers. Many students, including those in K–12 education as well as undergraduate and graduate students in higher education, experience AsP; this was especially true during the pandemic where access to personal contact and tutoring were and still are limited.

Academic Performance and the Pandemic

An alarming number of students failed their courses during the COVID-19 lockdown and the shift to online learning. OneClass conducted a survey of 14,000 college freshmen, sophomores, and junior students regarding their academic performance during the fall of 2020 (St. Amour, 2021). The news proved quite discouraging—a record 85% of students surveyed reported the pandemic negatively affected their academic performance (para. 3).

**"ACADEMIC STUDENT PROCRASTINATION"
- TRIAGE ASSESSMENT**

1. What are the reasons for the delay in completing assigned work?
2. What circumstances trigger the onset of this problem?
3. How has academic procrastination affected your life?
4. Do you ever experience negative feelings or emotions, such as anxiety, stress, guilt, or shame?
5. Please rate your level of discomfort or pain in your current situation from 1-10.

Figure 8.1. Triage Assessment in the Urgent Care Clinic.
Source: Created by Jessica Jo Noonan.

Students offered two reasons for the decline in their performance: "academic changes and mental health" (St. Amour, 2021, para. 5). Teachers reported that the problems associated with online learning contributed to student failure, including lack of access to equipment, decline in student engagement, and failure to submit assignments. The effects of a radical change in teaching and the learning environment as well as the isolation from others due to the pandemic likely exacerbated the conditions associated with AsP.

Steel and Klingsieck (2016) added the word "student" to the earlier term, *academic procrastination*, and shifted the focus away from the behavior to the actual problem: the lack of successful student progress toward completing academic tasks. Students with signs of AsP do not necessarily procrastinate in all academic areas or the other areas of their life. Viewed through another lens, the underachievement of college students during the pandemic (St. Amour, 2021) looks a lot like AsP and its effects on student performance.

In this chapter, a definition of AsP is followed by a description of the factors affecting student performance and well-being. The list of causes involves both the students and their learning experiences as well as the academic tasks and the level of support needed to complete the task. Most people do not need a definition of procrastination (to delay) because they may have experienced it under certain circumstances, such as tax preparation. Perhaps we know others who procrastinate and understand its detrimental effects.

Action Research: Academic Student Procrastination

Before beginning with a definition of AsP, an introduction to the informal and formal studies conducted to accumulate knowledge and experience about AsP follow. I discovered early in my career that student success depends on teacher success—what a revelation! Like most good teachers, I felt frustrated and disappointed with students who refused to engage in learning and seemingly asked for failing grades.

Initially, I privately made a list and divided academically underperforming middle school students into two groups: (1) students who did not know how to do what I asked them to do with their current knowledge and skills, and (2) students who possessed enough of the knowledge and skills needed to at least approach and potentially complete the task in a supportive learning environment.

The first group of students received strategy instruction and support and the second group of students spent many days after school in my private classroom study hall until they completed their assignments, again with support. Students in both groups needed different types of support. Over the years, I realized the process of dividing students into two groups was only the beginning. Understanding how students engage or disengage in learning based on a variety of factors raised my number of groups to the number of students in any class.

A cycle of action research often begins with a "nagging problem" in practice, such as disappointing graduation rates, low achievement test results, or the lack of student engagement in learning (Noonan, 2013). The problem increases teachers' level of awareness and concern, and may involve a single student, a group or cohort of students, or an entire program.

Action researchers conduct research "*from inside* . . . [a social setting to make] an immediate impact on practice through its integral connection to day-to-day work" (Nofke & Somekh, 2011, p. 95, italics in original). The nagging problem in my action research study concerned students likely to end their degree program as "noncompleters" (Lovitts, 2008).

My review of literature produced well over 15 factors associated with AsP in doctoral education, ranging from fear of failure and disengagement (Alexander & Onwuegbuzie, 2007) to interactions with peers and peer support (Barnett, 2008). I collected and analyzed data, which included interviews, observations, documents, and completion rates over the three phases of action research and used critical reflection to discover the most viable solutions to AsP.

I later interviewed program graduates regarding the efficacy of various interventions and their "recovery" from AsP. In the next two chapters I describe "how I [learned and] know what I know" about students in higher education (Patton, 2014, p. 382). The ages and types of developmental challenges differ, but the general causes of AsP remain similar. This chapter defines and then describes the factors affecting the onset of AsP. The next chapter describes prevention, intervention, and recovery pedagogies. The definition of AsP and the risk factors affecting the likelihood of AsP appear next.

This chapter does not address program quality, a significant factor influencing student outcomes. A discussion of program quality as well as strategies for interrupting and combating AsP appear in the next chapter. The focus of this chapter is on the student learning and performance and the six factors to consider when diagnosing AsP. Before beginning with the causes, however, a definition of a special type of procrastination, namely academic *student* procrastination, deserves attention.

DEFINING ACADEMIC STUDENT PROCRASTINATION

Steel and Klingsieck (2016) defined academic student procrastination (AsP) as a decision "to voluntarily delay an intended course of *study-related action* despite expecting to be worse off for the delay" (emphasis in the original; p. 37). A variety of reasons exist regarding the cause and circumstances favoring the likelihood some students, even highly successful students, may experience some level of AsP during their academic careers.

Understanding AsP may help professors and teachers to recognize the early signs of AsP and support students headed for academic problems. Several phrases found in the definition of AsP deserve attention. For example, a "voluntary decision" implies a conscious or deliberate choice (Steel & Klingsieck, 2016). Confident teachers may view students' voluntary decision to delay as temporary and subject to change under certain circumstances—including their intervention. Professors know a serious case of AsP becomes a self-defeating habit—easy to acquire and difficult to discard.

Next, Steel and Klingsieck's (2016) definition of AsP focused on a "*study-related action*" (p. 37). When procrastination takes hold, students with AsP reduce their chances of success and the class loses a valuable contributor. Students experiencing AsP may not engage in class discussions, contribute to group work, complete assignments, or take the necessary steps needed to complete a major research paper, project, or performance. Students' lack of authentic participation stands out to teachers and professors and peers. Negative emotions, including shame, guilt, and sorrow accompany AsP.

Turning around a voluntary decision to "delay" should occur as early as possible before the likelihood of course or degree completion decreases and adverse consequences increase. The phrase, "expecting to be worse off for the delay," means students expect some trouble but often underestimate the true cost of postponement (Steel & Klingsieck, 2016, p. 37).

Another hidden cost of AsP involves student development. While the external evidence of AsP might be a failing or incomplete grade, the internal and invisible cost to students concerns the lost opportunities to continually develop and flourish as students and human beings. Students struggling with AsP predictably experience a lack of academic progress and personal growth. This includes the experiences leading to deep learning, changes in identity, critical awareness of others, and transformation of self.

Limited engagement in learning leads to a decline of academic knowledge and skills as well as missed opportunities to learn something well. Students often think they can make up an assignment to quickly get back on track. They may be right, *if* the subject matter is easy, *if* the content and/or skills do not involve an iterative process, *if* the professor accepts a late assignment, and *if* students overcome the same behavior causing them to disengage in the first place.

Students may fall behind fast and struggle in advanced coursework without the predictable gains expected in a program of study. Missing one assignment and deadline does not necessarily warrant a diagnosis of AsP. However, a steady pattern of incomplete or late work may eventually lead to consequences associated with AsP—namely the failure to understand and complete academic tasks. A demanding course or program may soon dispel students' naïve views regarding their ability to complete a large project without steady work, formative feedback, and learning with others.

A large paper, project, or presentation poses predictable challenges for all students, even students with admirable academic track records. Students who lack the resources, such as time to make progress, the positive support of others, and coaching from their professors may find themselves unable to succeed even with effort.

When students, even formerly very successful students, do not or cannot successfully complete the assigned work, they often resort to subterfuge. They hide their lack of preparation and understanding of the course content in class meetings. The lack of preparation and engagement in class meetings may cause students to postpone attempts to complete projects and papers, offer reasons for the delay, make promises they cannot keep, and hope they can find a way to figure out how to do it.

Why do students expect to be "worse off" because of their voluntary decision to delay and continue to avoid academic tasks despite the costs associated with delay? The decision seems irrational because it is irrational (Bridges & Roig, 1997). Delaying the pursuit of academic goals and degrees becomes more consequential with each passing day, week, or year. If the window for degree completion passes, students may find themselves dismissed from the program with no degree and saddled with substantial debt.

Students often experience more than one reason for the problems associated with AsP. To identify the root causes of AsP, professors and teachers may use a diagnostic approach to initially understand students' struggles and then figure out what and how factors affect students' academic performance.

FACTORS AFFECTING ACADEMIC STUDENT PROCRASTINATION AND PERFORMANCE

When students begin a new semester or academic year, they enter class with hope, regardless of their past academic performance. Students assess their chance of success and decide early in the course regarding whether putting in effort may lead to success. "There are two aspects of achievement motivation, hope of success (HS) and fear of failure (FF)" (Schultheiss & Brunstein, 2005, p. 15). Fear of failure exerts greater influence on engagement than the hope for success. Students wish to avoid the negative feelings and loss of face associated with failure and they hide their lack of competency.

Students assess their competence as they review the course syllabus and note the expectations, learning activities, and projects. Students may quickly assess whether they possess the knowledge, desire, and ability to engage the academic tasks required. Sources of "motivation energy" may include student interest in academic tasks and estimates of their ability to complete the task (Schultheiss & Brunstein, 2005, p. 35).

When the level of *motivational energy* needed matches the appropriate task with the desirable level of difficulty (not too difficult or too easy), students may more readily attempt to complete a task (Schultheiss & Brunstein, 2005). Successful completion of an academic task increases competence, giving students an opportunity to experience positive emotions regarding their accomplishment. Learning increases competence—an essential resource needed to fight the "fear of failure" and replace it with the "hope of success" (p. 15).

Students' readiness and ability to succeed in a program or course may be affected by one or more of the following seven factors:

- Relationships and the Learning Environment
- Prior Learning Experiences and Academic Performance
- Engagement: Task Interest or Aversion
- "Learning-to-Learn" Knowledge, Skills, and Dispositions
- Gaps in Education and Learning Loss
- Roles and Responsibilities
- Major Life Events

The factors favoring AsP likely look familiar to most teachers and professors with even a few years of experience. During the pandemic quite a few students experienced "learning loss" due to the pivot to online learning and decline in student engagement. Competing roles might make participation impossible with additional roles beyond the role of "student." The hours devoted to paid employment compete with the time needed to study and complete assignments. Student and employee identities both require time and energy.

The factors affecting AsP sometimes combine and may adversely affect student performance, creating barriers that interfere with their success (see figure 8.2). The factors begin with relationships and the learning environment because this factor accounts for students' willingness to engage based on their relationship with their professor and peers.

Relationships and the Learning Environment

When students enter the classroom for the first time (either on campus or online), they look for ways to establish or renew relationships in a new learning space. Students want to feel safe and fully included and know someone sees and cares about them. Samuel (2017) identified and succinctly defined three fundamental elements necessary to create a caring classroom, which included respect, recognition, and reciprocity:

Figure 8.2. Seven Factors Affecting Academic Student Procrastination.
Source: Created by Jessica Jo Noonan.

    Respect means that students know that their voices and experiences are valued and heard (Samuel, 2017). Recognition means that everyone is seen and accepted for who they are, as a whole person—not just a number or a grade, but an individual whose unique differences are welcomed. Based on Samuels's (2017) description, recognition involves being seen, known, and valued. Finally, reciprocity occurs when students realize the value of everyone's contribution results in individual and group gain.

    All students need to feel respected, recognized, and valued as co-contributors in the learning environment. Diverse learners may enter the class with a sense of weariness, and look for teacher confirmation of their identity. Diverse students look for curriculum that reflects and values their culture. The root causes of academic student procrastination may be due to systemic bias and discrimination, lack of access to resources, or gaps in education or learning loss.

The factors affecting student performance can become questions. For example, "To what degree do relationships and the learning environment welcome and engage diverse learners?" "How do prior learning experiences affect student engagement and academic performance?" Understanding the causes of academic student procrastination provides ideas about how to support students to ensure they raise their level of achievement and confidence.

Positive and enjoyable teacher-student-peer relationships seem an obvious source of positive energy and enjoyment as well as a tool for academic achievement. Even the physical space affects relationships by making it easy to see and know peers, form groups, work in teams, and interact with teachers and professors. So many factors affect students' learning experience and chances of success (and avoidance of AsP).

The learning environment includes high quality relationships, active learning, and the strong bonds found in a true community of learners. Students and teachers appreciate positive, welcoming, and inclusive learning environments with opportunities for success in large part due to strong relationships.

Even if all factors seem ideal, there are other reasons why otherwise productive students might experience AsP. Prior learning experiences and academic performance, including previous failed attempts and successes get carried into the next class. Prior academic performance affects student decisions about the next course and their anticipated and actual success on learning tasks. Academic performance makes the completion of the next learning task possible.

PRIOR LEARNING EXPERIENCES AND ACADEMIC PERFORMANCE

Visualize a student entering a classroom carrying or wearing an "academic" backpack. Look inside. The backpack contains the academic tools needed to experience success as well as a detailed record of students' prior learning experiences. An expandable portfolio of artifacts in the backpack reveals the student's highest level of development and achievement. Report cards and transcripts show the types of courses attempted and passed.

Other measures of academic performance, such as test results and completion of student projects, papers, and presentations reveal capabilities and talents. The information inside the academic backpack provides evidence of students' learning history to date. Students know what's inside their backpack, including areas of strong and weak performance, and their assessment of the contents initially affects their participation in learning.

The factors affecting academic student procrastination and performance begin with students' "self-evaluation" of the backpack contents and their "attitudes about education" carried into the next course (Cross, 1981, p. 124). The backpack includes the students' prior learning experiences, level of engagement, and actual academic achievement and accomplishments.

Additionally, the academic backpack holds knowledge and evidence of students' strengths and capabilities, interests, talents, and personal qualities that support learning. Students' learning history and achievements act as either motivators or de-motivators for participation and attempting a new academic goal or task (Cross, 1981). The explanation for this seems obvious but plays an important role in student engagement in learning:

> Specifically, the research suggests that persons who lack confidence in their own abilities (frequently termed failure threatened or deficiency oriented) avoid putting themselves to the test and are unlikely to volunteer for learning which might present a threat to their sense of self-esteem. (p. 125)

Prior achievement affects students' estimate of their likely success or struggle in a new course. Students estimate whether their attempts to complete learning tasks are likely to go well or end in failure. They ask themselves this question: "Can I do this?" If the answer is "No" or "Doubtful," students avoid the risk of failure and embarrassment and look for a remedy. This might include dropping a course or even worse, leaving school.

Levels of achievement determine whether students' appraisals of the learning task fall within the range of possibility or appear highly unlikely. Unfortunately, students may fail to consider how skilled and dedicated teachers may provide the support needed to help them accomplish an academic goal. Achieving professors assume students can learn and address the gap in learning related to the academic task with direct intervention, ongoing support, and positive relationships.

Sometimes students can do something well, even enjoy accomplishing a goal, but at other times they avoid the task because they strongly dislike what they are asked to do. The difficult assignment may get postponed until the last minute because students cannot do the task, or they refuse to complete the task despite the penalty imposed for non-completion. Students' level of task interest or aversion affects AsP.

ENGAGEMENT: TASK INTEREST OR AVERSION

Types and levels of student interest influence their engagement in learning and academic performance. "[The] relationship between interest and learning has focus on three types of interest: individual, situational, and topic" (Ainley et al., 2002, para. 4). Individual interest involves a predisposition toward learning something interesting. The benefit to this type of interest involves a bonus for teachers and students—students want to learn, and they enjoy the process. The topic, not the teacher, influences the motivation to learn.

Situational interest differs from individual interest because it depends on the more immediate circumstances to sustain interest (Ainley et al., 2002). Interest depends on the content and the way learning activities and events are presented and organized (Ainley et al., 2002). If the task design and learning activities prove engaging, the interaction associated with a situational interest might eventually lead to genuine individual interest.

Novelty, challenges, choice, and/or peer collaboration foster student engagement in learning. "When students become fascinated with a topic, much like the 'individual interest' described earlier, they become more engaged because they value the content or process of learning" (Ainley et al., 2002). Teachers' interest and passion for a topic raise student interest—the teacher's excitement can be contagious.

One important cause of procrastination, perhaps hidden in the shadow of curriculum topics and assignments, involves "task aversion" (Afzal & Jami, 2018). When students strongly dislike what they are asked to do, their normal resources for completing work simply slip away. They delay or avoid tackling an assignment or project because tempting and competing alternatives to working on the dreaded task easily win. Interest raises engagement, and task aversion reduces it.

Assessing the worthiness of projects and assignments involves considering whether students will gain important knowledge and skills as well as enjoy some aspect of the assigned task. Some students may overcome their dislike of the task because of the greater reward on its completion, including a degree, a profession, or even the satisfaction of achieving a goal.

A very difficult project strikes fear in the heart of students overwhelmed by a complex, long-term project. Students may lack a strategy to organize the project, struggle with understanding the process for completing the task, and/or lack routine and scholarly habits to complete academic work. Fear of failure or dread halts the forward motion students need to start, continue, and complete a project due to their lack of academic self-regulation.

Pekrun (2006) described boredom as "a deactivating emotion [which] has deleterious effects on students' intrinsic and extrinsic motivation to learn, and academic achievement" (as cited in Tam et al., 2020, p. 125). Conversely, task interest is associated with positive emotions, including enjoyment and pride in accomplishment (Villavicencio & Bernardo, 2013).

When students describe a highly favorable learning experience, they often share stories about their interest in the topic or problem solving as well as their interest in learning with their peers. "The positive relationship between self-regulation on student learning is actually contingent on the student's experiencing positive emotions during the learning activities" (p. 331). College students noted one way to mitigate boredom involves the way professors made a lecture interesting based on their "personal attributes, qualities, and teaching strategies" (Tam et al., 2020, p. 126).

Students may respond favorably to the engaging task; however, their estimations of success still influence their level of engagement. Students assess and evaluate their chances of success early into the course, even the first day. Entering the next level challenge with the learning-to-learn skills needed affects whether participation and engagement may increase or a gradual pattern of AsP takes hold.

Villavicencio and Bernardo (2013) described enjoyment as an "academic emotion related to the process of learning, whereas pride is a retrospective emotion that relates to some previous outcomes of learning processes" (p. 329). Students' level of learning to learn knowledge, skills, and dispositions (KSD) affect their capacity and willingness to engage in the next level work.

"LEARNING TO LEARN" KNOWLEDGE, SKILLS, AND DISPOSITIONS (KSD)

To complete an academic project, students use their learning-to-learn knowledge, skills, and dispositions gained from previous learning experiences and use this knowledge to tackle the next challenging task. Some examples of KSD include knowing and using critical and creative thinking skills and problem-solving methods, searching databases to locate scholarly studies, and identifying the themes of human experience found in fiction and nonfiction texts.

Levels of KSD can be general as well as discipline specific. Learning-to-learn skills involve both the cumulative knowledge gained from academic success and failure as well as the increasing skill acquired in tackling and finishing projects to an appropriate standard.

Once students experience learning difficulties and calculate whether they can experience success in completing the assignment or think they may not find success due to their current state of academic know-how, their level of engagement may drop; this might signal the beginning of academic student procrastination. A timely intervention may turn things around unless struggling students hide their problem to avoid the loss of face.

Academic self-regulation involves the ability to set and achieve goals as well as the control of the process used to achieve goals and the methods used to assess the progress toward completing a goal. "Pintrich (2003) describe[d] self-regulation as an active and constructive process where the learner . . . defines the goals of the learning tasks, and also monitors, regulates, and controls the cognitive and motivational processes towards attaining the goals" (as cited in Villavicencio & Bernardo, 2013, p. 331).

Two things favor self-regulation—a great-looking task and a positive learning experience while in pursuit of an advanced goal (Villavicencio & Bernardo, 2013). Positive emotions, such as enjoyment and pride, affect the degree of self-regulation possessed by learners and the level of academic success as measured by grade point averages (Villavicencio & Bernardo, 2013).

Learning-to-learn skills build with each successful completion of academic or professional tasks found within disciplines and/or fields. The "knowing what and how" extracted from one experience provides some of the tools needed to complete the next project. Learning-to-learn skills, viewed from disciplinary perspectives, involve specific processes and patterns of thinking to acquire knowledge. Patterns of thinking and vocabulary unlock the interior of the discipline, making it more accessible to learners.

Students learn about a discipline doing the real work of a professional in the field, becoming scientists, historians, or artists. If learning episodes or events lack the possibility of receiving explicit instruction on the patterns and language of the discipline, the general learning-to-learn knowledge and skills fall short. When students experiment with central concepts and processes, patterns of thinking and language become more integrated and transferable to another project.

Dispositions, defined as "the tendency of something to act in a certain manner under given circumstances," affects academic performance (Merriam-Webster, n.d., "Disposition," para.1). Examples of dispositions toward completing academic work include persistence, curiosity, problem solving, resourcefulness, and self-regulation. Certainly, some level of self-efficacy is needed to seek an advanced degree and devote the effort required to reach program completion.

Developing the habits of a scholar takes time to grasp and grow. For example, when scholars read a book, they move past "elementary" or basic reading, and often read, analyze, and mark the content simultaneously (Adler & Van Doren, 1940/1972). Marking the text in certain ways supports the retrieval of central points and passages for later use.

Advanced readers possess a lot of strategies but may not know how to explain what they do. Professors expose the methods to support all readers with detailed descriptions of strategies and strategy practice. Even the most academically talented students appreciate learning a new strategy (that's what made them successful in the first place). Learning-to-learn knowledge, skills, and dispositions affect the degree of effort and the distance possible in completing academic projects.

A short lesson on how to do something—even getting started—supports students when their level of knowledge and experience is inadequate to the task. When students procrastinate and avoid beginning or completing a project, they often lack the knowledge or strategy needed to do the work, or possess the habits required in scholarly work. This may be explained by a gap in their education or learning loss.

GAP IN EDUCATION AND/OR LEARNING LOSS

A gap in education involves students' lack of knowledge or achievement related to an anticipated or expected level of performance. Disruptions in formal education or the lack of a quality education both serve as reasons for the gap. A gap may exist because the sequence or program of study was presented in a haphazard manner or important knowledge and skills never made their way into the curriculum or the teacher's lesson plans.

Educational gaps also occur due to program interruptions caused by an extended illness, high student mobility (changing schools or housing), poor attendance, or arriving at school consistently late. Gaps exist due to the presence of implicit bias exhibited by teachers and administrators who make pro-White decisions involving student discipline (Gullo & Beachum, 2020). A disciplinary decision adversely affects students of color because the corrective action typically involves their removal from class, causing interruptions and disruptions of formal education.

An education gap might exist regarding the lack of exposure of advanced coursework, reducing the opportunities available for undergraduate or graduate education. A high school degree does not guarantee academic success in college coursework. Some institutions require students to enroll in remedial courses with zero credit in preparation for "real" college.

The negative emotions associated with the remedial requirement affects students' college experience. Clearly, students' lack of confidence in their abilities coupled with negative emotions does not favor academic achievement. The loss of opportunity to learn something in a sequential manner adds up in time, predictably causing students to get further behind and more likely to disengage from learning.

A gap in education means students never encountered essential concepts and skills, however, a learning loss means students once learned academic content and skills but no longer recall the important aspects of the content. More recently, estimates of "learning loss" accrued during the pandemic and caused many to worry about the educational "long haul" effects of poor schooling on students during the COVID-19 pivot to online learning.

The term "long haul" education here refers, in this case, not only to the difficulty in completing academic tasks but also the effort required to "relearn" academic skills The process involves remediation strategies and extended support to return students to expected academic performance. "The term **learning loss** refers to any specific or general loss of knowledge and skills or to reversals in academic progress, most commonly due to extended gaps or discontinuities in a student's education" (bold in the original; *The Glossary of Education Reform*, 2013, para 1).

Likely some gaps in education and learning losses occurred over the last two years (two years of the pandemic beginning in 2019)—widening the gaps in education that already existed between advantaged and disadvantaged students. A colleague once described a feeling of knowing something but not knowing it well enough to participate as a blinking light. Imagine a light switch that is turned on and off repeatedly. Part of the image is revealed during a second or two of light but is not on not long enough for the viewer to recall most details with accuracy. Students attempt to fill in the blank spots but may find themselves truly stuck due to the experience of not seeing and learning something well.

Learning loss leads to the reduction of "learning" to do as well as "learning-to-learn" knowledge, skills, and dispositions. An extended period without practice may explain some learning loss. A long involuntary delay presents the same or similar challenges as those experienced by students still attending class but stalled out due to a prolonged period of academic procrastination. Everyone has the same problem—they do not know how to get started and what to do next.

The effects of a delay or interruption in education results in a noticeable "gap." The negative academic emotions experienced by discouraged and ill-prepared students inflict pain on students' core identities. Students with learning loss often find themselves with a more doable challenge than those with a significant gap in education. Sooner or later students with a learning loss recognize a pattern they once learned and may catch up to their peers or colleagues. Observing their peers discuss and attempt a task may help students recall the absent content or process.

Assessing the degree and depth of a gap in education and/or learning loss allows professors and teachers to determine the types of intervention needed to complete academic tasks with similar effort and quality as their peers. Other factors, such as roles and responsibilities and life events, potentially increase the likelihood of AsP. The expectations of others placed on students may cause some students to determine whether progress even seems possible under certain circumstances.

STRESS OVERLOAD AND ROLES AND RESPONSIBILITIES

Meeting the demands of all the roles and responsibilities in our lives sometimes seems impossible. Like the rest of us, students play other roles, including employee, athletic team member, friend, partner, parent, provider, caretaker, volunteer, veteran, and/or family member. While this seems an obvious point, the number and types of roles and responsibilities might explain the root cause of AsP for some overwhelmed students. An unexpected or critical life event typically accounts for additional role stress.

For example, students may suffer unemployment, defeat on the playing field, undergo treatment for serious illnesses, experience change in valued relationships, and/or see an increase in the care needs of a vulnerable family member. Time and energy drop precipitously with excessive and competing role demands. Examples of factors affecting the degree and controllability of role demands and responsibilities illustrate how some modifications may be made, while other demands appear unrelenting. Role types and responsibilities factor into whether students figure out how to juggle the role demands or eventually experience AsP because devotion to academic success not only seems impossible, it is impossible!

You might ask students to write all their roles and responsibilities on a paper plate (or virtual image) and discuss what's on their plate right now and describe how they are managing their role demands.

One obstacle involves the time and support needed to meet academic performance standards and at least some of the role responsibilities. Attending school is a balancing act between the demands of the academic world and other competing, and often equally valuable roles. What other roles do students and faculty play that affect their opportunities for success? One or more roles compete for time and energy and may change overnight.

Students and faculty learn to balance the demands of everyday living until one or more roles overwhelms them. While some students manage role stress or stress overload well, others might experience a major or critical life event and disengage from the educational process. The final factor influencing AsP involves the emotional toll and adaptation needed due to unexpected life events.

MAJOR LIFE EVENTS

Whether positive and/or negative, life events potentially challenge academic roles and responsibilities and may slow or even halt academic progress. Some events meet the definition of a "major life event" because the event requires the commitment of substantial time and/or resources. Harkness and Monroe (2016) defined major life events as "environmental changes that have a definable beginning point in time and that would be expected to be associated with at least some degree of psychological threat, unpleasantness, or behavioral demands" (p. 729).

When something unexpected happens, students feel pressure and look for a way to cope with the event to reduce stress. Even planned events surprise students because they underestimated the time needed to address the demands of school and life. Sometimes students decide to interrupt their academic program to manage their lives. A long involuntary delay due to a life event results in nearly the same or similar challenges as students stalled out due to a prolonged period of academic procrastination.

While the reasons for delay differ, the effect of the delay includes gaps in students' education as well as learning loss. Students need professional help for both an assessment of the level and degree of emotional distress as well as the academic concerns caused by AsP. An educational assessment provides the information needed to diagnose the problem experienced by students and arrange some positive experiences to raise students' "self-efficacy" (Bandura, 1977).

SELF-EFFICACY AND LEARNING

Bandura's (1977) theory of self-efficacy involves the behavioral change needed when students experience stress. Bandura theorized self-efficacy is influenced by the "expectations of personal efficacy [, which] determine whether coping behavior will be initiated, how much effort will be expended, and how long it will be sustained in the face of obstacles and aversive experiences" (Bandura, 1977, p. 191). Students need to experience some form of success to feel encouraged about their ability to learn and perform.

Bandura's (1977) description of self-efficacy offers at least three questions to be considered by mental health professionals:

1. Does the student use healthy coping strategies?
2. Does the student possess the resources needed to adapt to the situation?
3. Is it realistic to assume the student can sustain excessive demands over time without significant costs to personal goals and well-being?

A mental health professional helps students answer the above questions and decide what to do. Overwhelmed and stressed-out students often consider withdrawing from school or dropping a course as a remedy. While this seems like a quick fix, the costs to students might be greater than a targeted intervention created by a mental health professional and/or professor.

Concerned educators may recognize a troubled student with both academic and mental health problems. Professors respond with empathy and devise a plan to keep students engaged in learning. Continued engagement keeps the hope and the possibility of recovery alive. Dropping out of school, even for a semester, may delay program completion for more than one semester. The bill for the delay adds up due to the high emotional and financial costs incurred from a life event as well as a program interruption.

Mental health professionals counsel and support students to help students adapt to a new situation as well as cope with and understand their experiences and distress. Educators want students to stay on track to avoid a situation that offers few options for recovery. This involves continuing to stay engaged in learning and devoting at least some time to completing assignments.

Encouraging students to complete assignments and catch up with the class seems like an obvious solution, until more is known about students' circumstances. Professors may not know the depth of misinformation or confusion, the lack of skills needed in tackling assigned projects, and/or the fear and discouragement experienced by students because of the gap in their education.

The level and type of support students needed to "catch up" may exceed the resources professors believe they possess to help students in a meaningful way. While students may need some time off from academic work, the return to course mode should occur as soon as possible. Unfortunately, difficult circumstances end up stealing a lifelong dream and result in enormous financial and emotional costs unless something happens to divert a failing pattern of academic student procrastination.

Sometimes a prolonged period of AsP gets the attention and support from student affairs professionals and/or guidance counselors. However, professors and students bear the primary responsibility for navigating and negotiating the AsP problem related to student learning and achievement. Ignoring the problem and hoping things change rarely serves as an effective strategy to combat AsP. Many valid reasons exist why students postpone their studies, quite often due to circumstances beyond their control. The same academic problems appear, even though the reasons for a program interruption differ from student to student.

SUMMARY

Academic student procrastination is typically attributed to individual behavior and choice. I view AsP as an academic problem in need of a solution—the "problem" stands in the way of students' development and transformation.

Many studies attribute AsP to mental and emotional health. While these factors exist and influence student progress, empathetic professors see and understand vulnerability and do what they can to ensure students experience success in at least one area of their life they can control. No magic pill exists to treat academic student procrastination. However, strategies exist to reduce the prevalence of AsP in education by treating it with *academic therapy.*

REFERENCES

Adler, M. J., & Van Doren, C. L. (1972). *How to read a book* (Rev. ed.). Touchstone. Original work published 1940.

Afzal, S., & Jami, H. (2018). Prevalence of academic procrastination and reasons for academic procrastination in university students. *Journal of Behavioural Sciences, 28*(1), 51–69.

Ainley, M. (2006). Connecting with learning: Motivation, affect and cognition in interest processes. *Education Psychology Review, 18,* 391–405.

Ainley, M., Hidi, S., & Berndorff, D. (2002). Interest, learning, and the psychological processes that mediate their relationship. *Journal of Educational Psychology, 94,* 545–561. https://doi.org/10.1037/0022-0663.94.3.545

Alexander, E. S., & Onwuegbuzie, A. J. (2007). Academic procrastination and the role of hope as a coping strategy. *Personality and Individual Differences, 42*(7), 1301–1310.

Bandura, A. (1977). Self-efficacy: Toward a unifying theory of behavioral change. *Psychological Review, 84*(2), 191–215. https://doi.org/10.1037/0033-295X.84.2.191

Barnett, D. L. (2008). *Experiences influencing degree completion articulated by doctoral students in education administration. University of Louisville.* Electronic Theses and Dissertations. Paper 74. https://doi.org/10.18297/etd/74

Bridges, K., & Roig, M. (1997). Academic procrastination and irrational thinking: A re-examination with context controlled. *Personality and Individual Differences, 22*(6), 941–944. https://doi.org/10.1016/S0191-8869(96)00273-5

Cross, P. (1981). A*dult learners: Increasing participation and facilitating learning.* Jossey-Bass.

Gullo, G. L., & Beachum, F. D. (2020). Does implicit bias matter at the administrative level? A study of principal implicit bias and the racial discipline severity gap. *Teachers College Record, 122*(3), 1–28. https://doi.org/10.1177/016146812012200309

Harkness, K. L., & Monroe, S. M. (2016). The assessment and measurement of adult life stress: Basic premises, operational principles, and design requirements. *Journal of Abnormal Psychology, 125*(5), 727–745. https://doi.org/10.1037/abn0000178

Lovitts, B. E. (2008). The transition to independent research: Who makes it, who doesn't, and why. *Journal of Higher Education, 79*(3), 296–325.

Merriam-Webster. (n.d.). Disposition. In Merriam-Webster.com dictionary. Retrieved October 3, 2023, from https://www.merriam-webster.com/dictionary/disposition

Nofke, S. E. & Somekh, B. (2011). *The SAGE handbook of educational action research*. Sage.

Noonan, S. J. (2013). *How real teachers learn to engage all learners*. Rowman & Littlefield.

Patton, M. (2014). *Qualitative inquiry and evaluation methods: Integrating theory and practice* (4th ed.). Sage.

Samuel, K. (2017). Creating more caring university classrooms. *The Samuel Family Foundation*. https://www.brookings.edu/opinions/creating-more-caring-university-classrooms

Schultheiss, O. C. & Brunstein, J. C. (2005). An implicit motive perspective competence. In A. Elliot & C. S. Dweck (Eds.), *Handbook of Competence Motivation*, 32–51. Guilford Press.

St. Amour, M. (2021, January 5). Survey: Pandemic negatively affected grades this fall. *Inside Higher Education*. https://www.insidehighered.com/quicktakes/2021/01/05/survey-pandemic-negatively-affected-grades-fall

Steel, P., & Klingsieck, K. B. (2016). Academic procrastination: Psychological antecedents revisited. *Australian Psychologist*, *51*(1), 36–46. https://doi.org/10.1111/ap.12173

Tam, K. Y. Y., Poon, C. Y. S., Hui, V. K. Y., Wong, C.Y. F., Kwong, V. W. Y., Yuen, G. W. C., & Chan, C. S. (2020). Boredom begets boredom: An experience sampling study on the impact of teacher boredom on student boredom and motivation. *British Journal of Educational Psychology*, 90, 124–137. https://doiorg.ezproxy.stthomas.edu/10.1111/bjep.12309

The glossary of education reform for journalists, parents, and community members. (2013, August 13). Learning loss, para 1. https://www.edglossary.org/learning-loss/

Villavicencio, F. T., & Bernardo, A. B. I. (2013). Positive academic emotions moderate the relationship between self-regulation and academic achievement: Positive emotions, self-regulation, and achievement. *British Journal of Educational Psychology*, *83*(2), 329–340. https://doi.org/10.1111/j.2044-8279.2012.02064.x

Chapter 9

Prevention, Intervention, and Recovery Pedagogies to Disrupt Academic Underachievement and Procrastination

Sarah Noonan

> Life is difficult. This is a great truth, one of the greatest truths. It is a great truth because once we truly see this truth, we transcend it.
>
> —M. Scott Peck (1978/2003, p. 15)

Students and faculty might wholeheartedly agree with the first two sentences of Peck's (1978/2003) book on values and spiritual growth. Life is difficult when attempting to achieve a challenging, yet ultimately rewarding goal. Several qualities favor accomplishment of goals, including persistence, optimism, and curiosity.

Students may begin a course with confidence or trepidation or anything in between the two positions on the achievement continuum. However, once things get started, things change in unpredictable ways. Significant barriers, whether personal or academic, may derail the attainment of a goal. Even the most optimistic and accomplished students need help. We all need help.

This chapter focuses on the role faculty, individually, and collectively, play in both preventing academic student procrastination (AsP) and intervening as needed with a variety of remedies to support student learning and achievement. Intervention also includes an intensive assistance plan when students fail to experience success and disengage from learning.

Students do not stand up and loudly proclaim they cannot do something; they quietly remove themselves from the painful experience of failure.

Optimistic educators know they can teach students what they need to know by temporarily lending their knowledge and skills to their students. This does not mean faculty do the work for students. Lending knowledge and skills means teachers show students how to do something and explain how the next step connects to the final accomplishment of the big goal.

Once students get back on track, the final "recovery" phase involves the gradual release of faculty support leading to increased student autonomy. A discussion of preventative measures related to the causes of AsP leads this chapter because the ingredients needed to ensure student success must be present to provide predictable and meaningful routes to course completion and graduation. The best way to avoid AsP is to stop it in its tracks—or at least slow it down to avoid the short- and long-term adverse effects of AsP.

PREVENTION

Steel (2007) described procrastination as "a prevalent and pernicious form of self-regulatory failure that is not entirely understood" (p. 65). However, Steel and Klingsieck (2016) conducted a meta-analysis of 1,000 studies related to AsP nine years later and found greater agreement regarding the causes of AsP. Their search for psychological explanations of AsP found one central trait, namely "conscientiousness" (p. 36).

Steel and Klingsieck (2016) further explored the trait of conscientiousness by using three of Costa and McCrae's (1992) "conscientiousness facet scales" to flesh out a more expanded meaning of this trait. Costa and McCrae's facets included "need for order, self-discipline and achievement striving" (as cited in Steel & Klingsieck, 2016, p. 36). These findings were aimed primarily at counseling and mental health professionals to provide insight regarding how a significant personality trait affects performance (Steel & Klingsieck, 2016). See figure 9.1.

The academic consequences of conscientiousness can be understood. When students are disorganized, impulsive, and value other activities, such as social activities over completing academic tasks (a competing goal), they may be headed for AsP unless something disrupts the pattern of postponement. Completing academic tasks takes concentration, organization, multiple attempts at meeting a goal, and putting forth time and effort.

The psychological factors associated with AsP may lessen their impact with appropriate support from mental health professionals and/or academic programs and interventions.

Some students will likely struggle with organization and self-regulation, and efficient strategies should be taught as part of their course. The "habits" of scholars include established routines for getting organized, keeping track

Figure 9.1. Strategies to Bolster Academic Success.
Source: Created by Jessica Jo Noonan.

of notes and references, and marking texts to retrieve information. These skills can be taught and practiced.

Working with others in small groups helps students with a "failure in motivation" and the "lack of self-regulation" (Steel & Klingsieck, 2016). Students gain ground learning from and with others to complete a successful team project or investigation. Students who suffer from anxiety, even if the trait does not compare to the importance of conscientiousness (Steel & Klingsieck, 2016), need support from teachers and peers in positive, collaborative, and inclusive learning environments.

Based on teacher observations, student achievement data, and participation in learning activities, teachers may diagnose the stuck points in learning and offer strategy instruction. Effective teaching reduces student tendencies toward AsP because they get an extra boost of energy to stay engaged in learning by making measurable progress.

PROMOTE NURTURING RELATIONSHIPS AND COLLABORATIVE LEARNING

Teacher-student relationships (TSRs) remain a highly important factor in K–12 and higher education. Relationships are even more important to secondary students as compared to elementary students (Roorda et al, 2011). This remains true for college students too. Reyes et al. (2012) used the term *classroom emotional climate* (CEC), to refer to the "quality of social and emotional interactions in the classroom" (as cited in Grams & Jurowetzki, 2015, p. 82).

Classrooms with high CEC "are characterized by teachers who are aware and sensitive toward the academic and emotional needs and individual perspectives of their students and who show interest in them" (Grams & Jurowetzki, 2015, pp. 82–83). TSRs affect rates of student achievement in classes with high CEC. A description of the importance of relationships and the learning environment begins the preventative measures.

Learning involves some type of dialogue. This includes an internal dialogue with the author of a book or a character in a story. A learning conversation with others or ourselves leads to the greater understanding, sometimes even conceptual breakthroughs that transform us. The most predictable form of learning involves dialogue with peers and experts.

According to Mintz (2021), "traditional remediation generally doesn't work, but *corequisite remediation*—enrolling students in standard classes with support—does" (italics added; para.19). *Corequisite remediation* involves different types of support, including direct strategy instruction, learning centers with support staff, recording of "how to" demonstrations, and prompt feedback. As students make progress, they see it is possible to succeed and it fuels their motivation to learn.

Optimism plays a critical role in assuring students they enter the class as equals with different needs and get what they need to learn and do well. Students need reassurance that things will go well. However, reassurance must be accompanied by preventative actions before, during, and after students finish a major assignment. It's not enough to tell students they will do well, they must know it from their experience of learning well.

PRIOR LEARNING EXPERIENCES AND ACADEMIC PERFORMANCE

Prevention of academic student procrastination (AsP) requires knowledge a problem exists as well as the ability to change the course structure, sequence, and approaches to learning and teaching for one student, or perhaps an entire class or program. Students fear research projects and papers because of the academic rigor and high standards used to evaluate student performance.

One of the top preventative measures to support student success involves strategy instruction. Strategies involve the "how" in learning to think and accomplish tasks (including metacognition), self-assessment, and evaluation of progress. Teaching a strategy may involve several different types of methods, including a step-by-step process, and the use of analogies and metaphors to show related or like ideas and processes. Like putting one foot in front of the other, a step-by-step strategy process often yields a predictable result: student success.

Step-by-Step Strategies

Quite often students need support to not only write a formal paper but also revise their paperwork based on "professional" criteria. Next, *"procedural knowledge"* relates to the knowledge and expertise needed to select and apply strategies to attain a goal, described as "know-how" (Harris et al., 2010, p. 228). Individuals who know the right conditions to use procedural and declarative knowledge possess *"conditional knowledge"* (p. 228). The definitions offer insight with rereading the learning and teaching process. It's not enough to assess and describe the knowledge, skills, and strategies needed to achieve a goal (*declarative knowledge*), students also need *procedural knowledge* to perform the task and *conditional knowledge* to determine when to use a strategy.

Direct instruction of strategies needed to complete a task simplifies the goal and breaks down the steps involved in performance. For example, Harris et al. (2010) described a "revising strategy" which involves Compare (i.e., detect mismatches between the author's intensions and the actual written text), Diagnose (i.e., determine the cause of such mismatches), and Operate (i.e., decide what types of changes are needed and carry them out" (CDO; p. 14).

Using the CDO method, students read their text, sentence by sentence, and use index cards with ready-made evaluation notes and responses, such as "This doesn't sound right," or "Say more" (Harris et al., 2010, p. 248). Every step in the CDO is explicit and raises awareness regarding how to edit. The cards can be upgraded for advanced readers and writers. Revision requires the writer to assess writing in the role of reader, not writer. Should I say more?

STIR It Up: Analyzing and Interpreting Data

I developed a four-step mnemonic model of analysis called "STIR" it up. Basically, the procedure involves following a step-by-step-process: (1)

summarize the data;(2) select and describe a *theory* used to analyze data; (3) *interpret* data using one or more theories—working back and forth with the data and interpretation; and (4) *reflect* on the findings and *recommend* further research and action.

The "STIR It Up" strategy puts things in the right order and exposes the logic needed to analyze and interpret data. Students develop a table with the data on the vertical axis (phrases or themes) and the concepts that together form the theory on the horizontal axis. Once the table is created, students place an "X" in every cell that applies, and then they use all or part of the theory to explain, analyze, and interpret data.

Once this relationship is recognized (how theory proves useful to analyze experience), students make sense of their data by moving back and forth between a theoretical concept and the data. The construction of meaning and its application occurs through discovery and reflection. The "end" of the process occurs once recommendations are made to upgrade or change existing practices based on findings.

Strategy Discovery

A different approach to strategy instruction involves "strategy discovery," a process used throughout our lives to solve problems and become more efficient (Waters & Kunnmann, 2010). Strategy instruction and metacognition (thinking about thinking) go together. Strategy discovery helps students become more aware of the meaningful and efficient processes they use or invent to accomplish their work and gain knowledge.

To discover strategy, professors or teachers discuss the process used and the next step in the process, using students' thinking and actions to expose the strategy and in some cases, correct it. A strategy note gets written to refer to for the next time. Acquiring scholarly habits involves inventing and using strategies to make sense of the work, organizing materials, and selecting a process. Building a repertoire of strategies for academic and professional work supports student growth in learning how to become and be a scholar and professional.

The Power of the Spoken Word

Teachers often recommend students read their text out loud to hear their mistakes. However, students can also listen to their text using the "text-to-speech" command on their computer. The speaking command allows the writer to stop the text reading, fix a sentence, hear it read again, and when satisfied, accept the change, and continue. When students listen to their text, they typically feel good about their writing after a few edits and readings. The text-to-speech function, originally intended for visually impaired people, now benefits everyone. Introducing the spoken word exercise takes little preparation.

Before class started one day, I asked a student to volunteer their text for a class demonstration using the text-to-speech function on the computer for a demonstration. I promised to remove the student's name. I selected my favorite voice (look for settings) and, started class with the sound of the computer reading beautiful text. The debriefing included the benefits of the text-to-speech strategy and the way hearing the text revealed the "argument pathway" and the sound of engaging text. The students were spellbound, hearing the beauty of the language and realizing the power of listening to their text in the future.

When students learn a new strategy, they experience an "aha" moment. The new and improved strategy breaks down conceptually difficult theories or processes. Strategies give students the initial knowledge needed to open the previously locked door hindering their progress. Teaching students how to learn by adopting the habits of scholars prepares them for the accomplishment of more difficult tasks. To ensure students participate in learning, you might examine whether some of the assigned academic topics and tasks peak student interest or produce boredom.

TASK INTEREST AND AVERSION

Ainley (2006) distinguished between personal and situational interest. Personal interest, like personality traits, becomes part of the student's overall persona. When personal interests align with the course content and learning activities, students feel attracted to learning and sustain their engagement without a lot of support from teachers and even peers. The personal interest alone motivates them, and other attractive "situational" factors in the learning process serve as a bonus.

Situational interest occurs as a one-time event (Ainley, 2006; Frick, 1992). Students willingly participate in a learning activity because of novelty (e.g., simulation, role play, setting), a fascinating topic (e.g., Who shot John Kennedy?), or the processes or products involved (e.g., create a newspaper, construct a model, or curate a collection of protest images). Frick (1992) described the concept of interestedness as "a feeling of interest prior to learning an outcome of an event" (p. 1).

The interest may also continue after the event and later become a personal interest. Before students engage in a learning activity, Lazarus (1999) found students first evaluate whether the activity is interesting, and then determine whether they understand what is asked of them—its "comprehensibility"

(Silvia, 2008, p. 58). The two appraisals influence students' decision making regarding the type and level of their engagement or disengagement.

Task aversion predictably leads to reduced participation or disengagement in learning. Cross (1981) devised a "Chain of Response" (COR) model related to adult motivation to learn. Certain factors facilitated engagement or disengagement. Cross characterized the factors as decision points, which either encourage engagement or predict disengagement and departure sometimes from the activity or at other times the course.

The most interesting thing about the COR model (Cross, 1981) is that engagement can increase or decrease within the same hour or day. When students become keenly aware of their strong responses to the task, they make small decisions about their response to learning in real time. Another key factor influencing task interest or aversion involves whether learners have access to information and the support needed during the various stages of learning.

Students' prior achievement history and experiences influence participation. The COR model opened the idea of a decision-making chain: learners change from engagement to disengagement and back to engagement as learning conditions and students' estimate of success change (Cross, 1981).

One way to assure students they can do well in completing academic tasks involves directly teaching and modeling the knowledge, skills, and dispositions needed to sustain their engagement in learning. Trouble comes when students' initial attempts to progress toward an academic goal yield little to no result. Preventative measures to these circumstances involve the direct teaching of strategies and concepts and practice using the acquired knowledge. Boredom or disinterest may lead to task aversion; however, another cause involves asking students to do something they cannot do without your support.

"LEARNING TO LEARN" KNOWLEDGE, SKILLS, AND DISPOSITIONS

"Learning to learn" knowledge, skills, and dispositions (KSD) carry students through the learning process. Students often need and appreciate mini "refresher" lessons on the concepts, processes, or habits needed to manage conceptually difficult ideas and/or processes as they proceed through a course. The short mini lessons appear throughout the semester to address the likely shifts needed in their understanding. If possible, you can record the lessons and place them on a learning resources page.

Helping students use a more advanced and expert knowledge of the disciplines is part of the process in becoming and being a great student and scholar. As this begins to happen, students begin to change their identity from student to scholar. Professors offer strategy, feedback, and coaching to help students become more competent in their ability to do academic work. What's new in the next area involves the *added support needed to get students through a very difficult time*. Students know the gap exists and feel discouraged before they enter the class for the first time.

GAPS IN EDUCATION AND LEARNING LOSS

Gaps in education and/or learning loss typically thwart student success in completing academic tasks without greater intensive assistance. Instead of crossing a small stream to catch up with other students, students with a gap or loss in their education need a life jacket and boat to get to the other side. Recording instructional videos and providing accessible supplemental learning resources allows students to privately access the resources and return to them when they feel stuck.

Hattie (2015) describes the important role teachers play in adopting a flexible and strategic approach to helping students and, of course, disrupting AsP. One strategy involves *diagnosis, intervention,* and *evaluation* (DIE; p. 81). The three-step process gets repeated until students make enough progress on engaging the work and experiencing success.

The DIE model elegantly reveals a simple process in defeating AsP (Hattie, 2015). Evaluation pertains to not only the quality of student work but also the impact and effectiveness of the interventions used. Effective teachers evaluate their impact on students by considering the efficacy of their efforts. Evidence of student learning and transformation builds teacher self-efficacy (Grambow, 2021).

STRESS OVERLOAD AND ROLES AND RESPONSIBILITIES

When students enter high school or college at any level, they bring other roles and responsibilities with them. Roles come with obligations based on the responsibilities expected from others as well as what we expect of ourselves. Often roles do not get discarded, even though the role of student gets added to the other roles. Students experience certain types and amounts of role stress based other circumstances.

Amirkhan (2012) established the widely accepted description of "pathogenic stress" by defining this type of stress based on two factors that include "the interplay of two constructs, (1) demands and (2) resources" (p. 56).

Pathogenic stress occurs when high demands exceed the resources available to fulfill roles and responsibilities.

Amirkhan et al. (2022) found first-generation college students (FGCS) experience stress overload at greater rates than continuing-generation college students (CGCS). Employment and family responsibilities often play a significant role in contributing to the demands placed on students in addition to the role of student. Stress increases as the semester progresses.

After the half-way mark in a class, students typically take over more of the responsibility for their learning. Projects, presentations, and papers demand more of their most precious resources, namely time and energy. *Stress overload* (Amirkhan et al., 2022) grows during the second half of the course because demonstration and application of knowledge is expected.

Students conduct original research, complete case studies, write synthesis papers, and complete mid-term and final examinations. During the high-stress points in the semester, the weight of all the roles and responsibilities comes crashing down on the shoulders of already overloaded students.

Avoiding AsP in these circumstances may not be possible because professors lack control over the roles that compete for students' time. However, organizing a sequence of learning and schedule for production of large academic tasks reduces the large crash toward the end of the course and reduces stress.

Professors set due dates several weeks before the semester ends to reduce student stress and accommodate the work required in other courses. The added benefit involves fewer requests for extensions and grades of "incomplete." Students benefit from accessible supplemental resources because they may schedule a block of time to work only to realize they need more help.

Instead of tutoring students one by one, instructional videos benefit overloaded students. Every great instructional video essentially adds another class to the students' schedule. The videos educate students on what is required, how to accomplish the tasks, and the way a particular section or process contributes to the whole endeavor. The video serves as a patient teacher.

You can explain the project or paper in greater detail, review the guidelines, provide examples, and discuss typical problems or traps. The instructional videos and examples help students see the goal, processes, and examples that meet the standard. A section of the project or paper might be due weekly to cut the task down to size. Students share their drafts with their peers and compare their efforts to the work completed by others.

Other factors accounting for academic and health status concerns may be related to academic motivation, most notably the reason for earning a college degree. Próspero et al. (2012) found when students focus on the extrinsic goal of earning a degree to earn a better salary rather than the intrinsic goal of learning new ideas, the extrinsic rather than intrinsic goal is associated with lower grades (as cited in Amirkhan, 2022).

When students meet in small groups, they often discuss how they manage their time and responsibilities. Sometimes students create a "back channel" using social media to discuss their coursework and support each other's goals. Family expectations require a lot of time, and to gain time for a student role, some type of negotiation regarding "customary" roles is needed (Barnett, 2008). Closely tied to the pressure of roles and responsibilities is the occurrence of a major life event, which has the potential to halt student progress.

MAJOR LIFE EVENTS

Major life events concern unexpected or continuing events that compete with the time and resources needed for learning. Some major life events include change in health status, illness, death, and the subsequent losses associated with these events.

To the degree possible, you might encourage students to stay in school and request a program interruption or extension. Students who stay connected with their professors and peers often avoid an official withdrawal from school. Major "happy" life events occur too, such as a marriage, the birth of a child, or a one-time amazing activity. These events also need some flexibility and celebration.

Keep students engaged in class via Zoom and support teacher-student and peer relationships through frequent contact. Class recordings via Zoom keep students engaged with their teachers and peers. Perhaps the most important point here involves how you show empathy for the circumstances and encourage AsP students to avoid taking an "all or nothing" approach to meeting the current life challenge. When students successfully complete academic tasks, their success bolsters their confidence and personal self-efficacy increases (Bandura, 1977).

However, AsP may lurk in the background and an old habit may return. Under stress, the habits that challenge students seem to get worse. A poor strategy, like postponing the completion of academic tasks, may defeat very capable students. However, a successful learning process may lead to "incremental or transformational changes" in learning, including increased knowledge, skills, and dispositions (Mezirow, 2000, p. 22).

Bandura's (1977) theory of self-efficacy identified two factors influencing the initiation and persistence needed to achieve mastery of a task, which included "outcome expectancy" and "efficacy expectation" (p. 193). Outcome expectancy refers to the belief that completing a task is likely to lead to the accomplishment of a goal (the process makes sense), but perhaps more importantly, "efficacy expectation is the conviction that one can successfully execute the behavior required to produce the outcome" (degree of confidence in completing the task; p. 193).

Student estimates of their likely success affect their level of engagement and persistence in completing the task. Students may believe in a goal and process but still consider it unattainable (Bandura, 1977). Teachers find ways to ensure student success. Gains in student achievement increase self-efficacy. Nothing beats success except more success. What stands in the way of student success? What's going on?

WHAT'S GOING ON?

No magic pill exists to treat a serious case of academic student procrastination. Academic student procrastination is typically attributed to individual behavior and free will choices. What if AsP was considered an academic problem in need of a solution? Optimistic educators believe in students and themselves. Instructors and professors focus their attention on students to address concerns related to AsP.

A private conference held between a professor and student provides an opportunity to discuss the reasons interfering with the successful completion of academic tasks. Before discussing the concern regarding incomplete work or poor performance, the focus should be on student well-being. Faculty should avoid telling students about the remedies needed to address AsP based on a quick assessment of their concerns (intended as a helpful move) and, instead, ask students to tell their entire story without interruption or advice.

It's difficult to reduce the "tell" side of teaching and embrace the "ask" side focused on students. The shift allows students to tell their story the way they want to tell it. Their stories offer valuable clues about their disengagement from learning. When I ask students about what seems to interfere with their academic success, they tell me what I need to know to help them, and I believe them.

Maximize/Minimize the Value of the Learning Experience

Lakey (2020) described a group learning activity that calls for honesty and candor. A real or virtual white board is ready for student input after reflecting on three interesting questions. The first question "asks participants to recall ways that they have personally found work well when they made full use of a learning opportunity" (p. 14). The question pertains to the use of scholarly habits and self-regulation skills to *maximize* their learning experience.

The second question poses the real challenge because it requires an admission of habits typically kept hidden. The facilitator "asks for ways in which they [participants] have *minimized* the value of a learning experience" (Lakey, 2020, p. 14). Participants might share the way they manage stress, procrastinate, or take on other projects instead of taking full advantage of the learning experience.

The final question involves asking participants to share how they "pull themselves back into the maximizing mode" (Lakey, 2020, p. 14). Quite a few participants, including the facilitator, may hope to learn an effective method to get out of a mess and back on track. Once the master list gets shared, there might be some laughs, nods, and agreement about what students do to *maximize* as well as *minimize* learning opportunities.

This maximizing exercise involves the focus on student choice rather than a deficiency in students or teachers. The reasons for the diversion from learning tasks provokes a lot of discussion regarding the competing roles and responsibilities. Students discuss whether they adopt self-defeating habits threatening their success in college. Sometimes the type and intensity of academic emotions provide answers to the maximizing and minimizing questions.

Academic Emotions

Academic emotions play a starring role in the learning process because they affect achievement motivation, learner engagement, and academic performance (Pekrun, 2014). Pekrun et al. (2002) found the most frequently reported emotion was anxiety, which accounted "for 15% of 25% of all emotions reported in the study" (p. 93).

Students experienced anxiety due to their desire to achieve and worry about failing. Pekrun (2014; as cited in Jensen, 2015) grouped and described academic emotions into the following four categories:

> achievement emotions [which] relate to success and failure with activities (e.g., contentment, anxiety, frustration); epistemic emotions [which] relate to cognitive problems (e.g., curiosity, confusion, surprise and frustration); topic emotions [which] relate to the topics students work with (e.g., empathy); and social emotions which relate to teachers and peers (e.g., pride, shame, jealousy, love, compassion, social anxiety). (as cited in Jensen, 2015, p. 63)

Reviewing the list of academic emotions and academic student procrastination suggests several connections. *Achievement emotions* (worry about failure) and *epistemic emotions* (conceptual problems) appear when students struggle to grasp ideas or adopt processes. They express confusion over a multistep process and exhibit frustration when a project requires creativity and tolerance for ambiguity.

Topic emotions are involved when students investigate social problems or troubling history (or both) and *social emotions* may relate to the class culture and climate, and students' sense of belonging (Pekrun, 2014 as cited in Jensen, 2015), If the climate is healthy and the relationships are nurturing, a lot of things become possible.

The term "meta-emotions" refers to the way students experience and feel [and think] about their emotions (italics in original; Pekrun et al., 2002, p. 93). This awareness may offer anxious students a strategy to manage negative emotions. Like metacognition, awareness of thinking helps to generate the executive functions of the brain into figuring out what's happened and what to do next. *Meta-emotions* engage students in understanding and managing their feelings in a similar way. Discussing the feelings associated with learning may support students' self-awareness and coping strategies.

The interventions described in the next section address both the emotional components as well as the academic interventions used to address persistent, prolonged academic student procrastination. The types of intervention described in the next section are needed when students resist even your best efforts to teach and support them during an episode of AsP.

INTERVENTIONS FOR PROLONGED ACADEMIC STUDENT PROCRASTINATION AND DELAY

Academic student procrastination (AsP) stands in the way of students continued academic development and performance. When viewing AsP as an academic problem, different types of interventions may slow or arrest the downward spiral of incomplete work and failing grades. If you tried all the other remedies, you likely ended up in this section because the typical solutions failed to produce any real change. When student behaviors become entrenched, it's unlikely a quick fix exists to bring about change.

INTENSIVE ASSISTANCE AND RECOVERY PEDAGOGIES

During the early sections of this chapter, various strategies were described to reduce the likelihood of failure and bolster the confidence of students at predictable times when students have trouble. The phases of an intervention cycle follow a simple pattern: establish nurturing relationships; invite students to learn and give students hope, establish structure, set goals, and provide coaching (one-to-one direct teaching); and deliver "fast" feedback by reviewing and discussing student work in a weekly meeting or virtual session. Teach and record strategies used to solve a problem and then repeat the process.

NURTURING RELATIONSHIPS

Nurturing relationships serve as the most important factor leading to student growth. The placement of "Nurturing Relationships" in the center of a circle represents how the teacher-student relationship affects every aspect of recovery from AsP. Students need to trust their teachers and feel cared for as part of the intensive assistance process. Relationships begin with establishing trust and truly seeing and appreciating students as individuals. See figure 9.2.

All healthy relationships rely on some form of trust. To give and receive trust involves vulnerability, an expectation of empathy, and confidence in the reliability of partners. Students feel vulnerable until they receive empathy. Disrupting academic student procrastination requires nurturing relationships. Trust allows students to honestly share the gaps in their education or their struggle with self-regulation. Another factor involves the approachability of professors, which reflects a combination of the affective and support dimensions (Hagenauer & Volet, 2014). Because nurturing relationships support every aspect of the process, relationships are critical in the process of disrupting academic student procrastination.

AN INVITATION TO LEARN AND HOPE

The next strategy used to disrupt AsP (or any form of underachievement) involves extending the invitation to learn, which provides students with an opportunity to try again. The invitation raises students' hope for success. Haigh's (2011) definition of invitational learning involves four core principles: "respect for people and their differences, trust expressed through cooperation and a sense of community, optimism about the untapped potential contained within each learner and intentionality, which means taking those steps needed to create each learning invitation and to address it to each learner" (p. 300).

Some students never imagine a second chance might be possible. The burden of holding on to the negative emotions, such as shame, guilt, embarrassment, and disappointment, lifts and ends with progress. Now a lost dream may become a reality with students' commitment and concerted effort. The

Figure 9.2. Intensive Assistance and Recovery Pedagogies.
Source: Created by Jessica Jo Noonan.

possibility of help generates hope and gratitude. The next step must begin as soon as possible to take advantage of the positive response and gain some momentum.

STRUCTURE AND SELF-REGULATION

Establishing structure for learning includes prompt and routine communication, weekly meetings to jointly review progress on the academic task, providing mini lessons on strategy, setting goals, video recording of work sessions, and noting progress. During this period, you lend students some of your knowledge and skills until students grow into the role of a successful student and scholar.

When students establish and meet goals, they make incremental progress, and this eventually leads to students taking over the planning progress. Students assess the degree to which they make progress on the goals, evaluate the quality of work, and discuss the processes used to attain it. Students practice and acquire the habits of achieving students by attempting the tasks and receiving coaching and feedback.

After returning students to "course" mode (regular meetings with assignments), professors engage in collaborative learning to get started on the work. Measurable tasks due every week typically lead to steady progress. Structure provides a response and remedy to increase self-regulation skills and organize the learning process using a sequential approach. Supplemental (how-to) resources become an important source of backup during the gap between the last meeting and the next one.

COACHING AND GAINS IN STRATEGY, ACHIEVEMENT, AND SELF-EFFICACY

The act and art of coaching involves directing the learner to focus on established goals using a developmental approach. Coaches establish the next step and goal based on the learner's self-assessment, work accomplished, observations, and previous feedback and evaluation. Academic coaches do not need to teach every aspect of the course, just the knowledge and skills needed to help students progress and meet the next goal.

The goal of coaching is to reduce the number of unproductive and failed attempts by breaking down the task and/or project phases into manageable chunks. Although these strategies may seem obvious, the focus on only the next step (temporarily) increases the odds students will do well. Repetition notably serves students who seem stuck. Professors can continue presenting the strategy and the reasons for it by providing stories and illustrating how strategies work.

One of the most effective strategies to explain difficult concepts is to use metaphors and similes. For example, I often refer to reviewing theory and selecting one to use for analysis as "shopping" for theory. We discuss how to determine whether the selected theory elevates understanding of data.

The description of the task and how to perform it is introduced or reinforced using memorable stories. I describe a problem Student "A" experienced and how they solved it. Next, Student B . . . I then tell stories (ensuring confidentiality) that fit students' current stage in the learning process and how the strategy works.

To make tracks, students do not need to see every step to get to the end of the path. Instead, students need just enough information to know they will reach their goal by facing obstacles preventing their progress and overcoming them. The power of fast, specific feedback on student work increases student learning and their transformation from underconfident, reluctant students to fledgling scholars.

Dweck (2019) described the growth (not fixed) mindset, which involves the individuals' belief in their innate ability to learn and continue to grow. The fixed mindset limits engagement because students assume their intelligence is fixed, limiting students' view regarding what is possible. The growth mindset encourages students to stick to their goals and experience the benefit of a challenge with the knowledge they can do more.

FEEDBACK, GAINS IN LEARNING, TRANSFORMATION, AND A GROWTH MINDSET

Two types of feedback get entirely different responses. The first type involves feedback that explains a grade. The rubric gets marked and the points assigned lead to a grade. Stahl (2021) interviewed high school teachers and found students ignored the teacher's feedback because nothing changed the outcome. The second type of feedback offers a diagnostic approach to learning with the goal of improving learning through an iterative process.

Stahl (2021) found teacher feedback was more meaningful to students when instructors discussed the feedback with them. Teachers spend hours writing comments. If the comments do not require revision of the work, the effort is largely wasted. One strategy to reduce instructor's time but get something solid accomplished is a simple method: "show how and why on the fly."

You can quickly review student work before the online or on-campus meeting, develop an idea about the type of feedback needed, and then start the lesson. Together professors and students evaluate their work. Students write their ideas on the most current file shared with the instructor. The edited file with notes serves as the record of the meeting and becomes a launching point for revision and new work. Video recordings help students review how to improve their work before they move on to the next task. You can spend minimal preparation time and still provide what students need at this time in their development.

During one coaching session a student asked me to "code" with them, a process used to develop themes from participant transcripts in qualitative research. I readily agreed. After one page, the student said, "I can do this now, I get it!" A few minutes of time helped the student to get unstuck. The student adopted a "growth mindset," realizing prior learning and learning loss did not stand in the way of success (Dweck, 2019).

More might be said about the various methods used to meet diverse student needs, in this case, to combat academic student procrastination. You likely noticed a lot of these strategies relate to affective, supportive, and effective learning and teaching methods. Helping one student or small group provides ideas for strategy instruction for a much larger group of students. No matter who or how one teaches, new strategies emerge from the process. Like the curb cut, the modifications made, or strategy discovery helps not just persons with visual impairment but also anyone needing support to cross a street.

SUMMARY

This chapter focused on prevention and intervention and the recovery strategies needed to combat academic student procrastination. Nurturing relationships, which include the interaction between teachers, students, and peers, exert a very significant effect on the lives of students and their participation in learning. Once students receive an invitation to learn, their hope for success increases. Students accept the invitation because they trust you. The next strategy involves establishing a structure for learning to accomplish goals and increase students' self-regulation. Self-regulation refers to the student's capacity to plan, monitor, and evaluate performance.

The coaching process involves the direct teaching of knowledge and skills along with text or project work. Students must show their work, whether it's one paragraph or 20 pages. The process starts with their work and ends with goal setting for the next time. Fast feedback gives students knowledge about how they are progressing.

After time passes, students get closer and closer to the goal. As this happens the instructor knows it is time to gradually release dependence on them. You can reduce the meetings, agree to provide the same level of feedback all students receive, and continue to support student success through nurturing relationships. All students should be visible, included, and appreciated as people worthy of respect and aware of their capabilities and talents.

Few students appreciate the true cost of AsP on their future. This includes psychological losses like decline of self-esteem and self-efficacy. A setback in one area of life might spill over to other areas with a cascading effect, lowering risk-taking and feelings of capableness and confidence. Providing different types of support helps to retain students who would otherwise leave school without some type of intervention.

Both as a preventative measure and a strategy to address stuck points in learning or academic student procrastination, the strategies on the outer circle in figure 9.3 bolster student learning and achievement. The inner circle presents some underlying causes and concerns that explain some of the reasons for academic student procrastination and underachievement. More than one concern may be present, and more than one type of support may be needed to help struggling students.

This chapter primarily emphasized the role played by faculty in both preventing AsP as well as intervening when students fail to find success. The strategies and practical applications provide ways to help students to reengage in learning, experience success, and recover from AsP. A successful recovery from AsP results in incremental changes in learning knowledge, skills, and habits. If all goes well, students learn what to do, how to do it, and why it's important to finish.

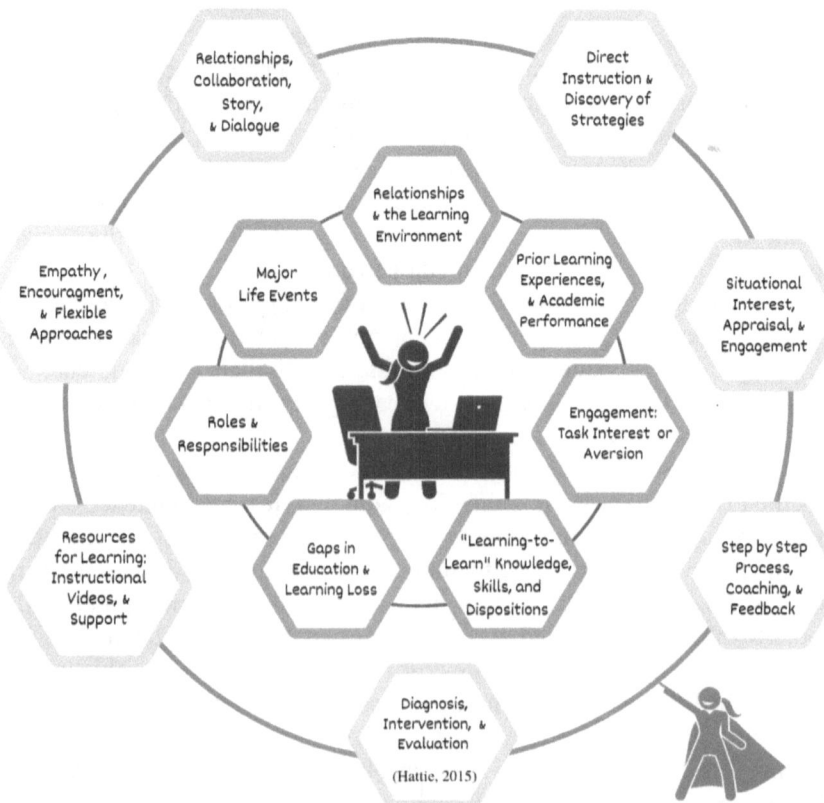

Figure 9.3. Academic Student Procrastination—Prevention and Intervention Strategies.
Source: Created by Jessica Jo Noonan.

A successful intervention not only helps students to complete an academic task, but also the accomplishment may *change the way individuals view themselves*. Cohen described how the process of identity change works: "Over time a series of these transformations in point of view about oneself as a learner ('I can understand these ideas') may cumulatively lead to a transformation in self-concept ('I am a smart, competent person')—a habit of mind" (as cited in Mezirow, 2000, p. 21). Students and professors change themselves by engaging in the learning process—this is the only way transformative learning can happen and be real.

REFERENCES

Ainley, M., Hidi, S., & Berndorff, D. (2002). Interest, learning, and the psychological processes that mediate their relationship. *Journal of Educational Psychology, 94*(3), 545–561. https://doi.org/10.1037/0022-0663.94.3.545

Amirkhan J. H. (2012). Stress overload: A new approach to the assessment of stress. *American Journal of Community Psychology, 49*(1–2), 55–71. https://doi.org/10.1007/s10464-011-9438-x

Bandura, A. (1977). Self-efficacy: Toward a unifying theory of behavioral change. *Psychological Review, 84*(2), 191–215. https://doi.org/10.1037/0033-295X.84.2.191

Barnett, D. L. (2008). Experiences influencing degree completion articulated by doctoral students in education administration. Electronic Theses and Dissertations. Paper 74. https://doi.org/10.18297/etd/74

Cross, P. (1981). *Adult learners: Increasing participation and facilitating learning.* Jossey-Bass.

Dweck, C. (2019, May). David Myers distinguished lecture on the science and craft of teaching psychological science. *Association for Psychological Science.* 2019 Annual Convention, Washington, DC. https://www.psychologicalscience.org/observer/dweck-growth-mindsets

Frick, R. (1992). Interestingness. *British Journal of Psychology, 83*(1), 113.

Grambow, D. (2021). *Teachers who thrive: Navigating the self-efficacy career journey.* Rowman & Littlefield.

Grams, S., & Jurowetzki, R. (2015). Emotions in the classroom. In B. Lund, & T. Chemi. *Dealing with emotions: Pedagogical challenge to innovative learning,* 81–98. Sense Publishers-Rotterdam, The Netherlands. https://doi.org/10.1007/978-94-6300-064-2

Hagenauer, G., & Volet, S. E. (2014). Teacher–student relationship at university: An important yet under-researched field, *Oxford Review of Education, 40*(3), 370–388, DOI: 10.1080/03054985.2014.921613

Haigh, M. (2011). Invitational education: Theory, research and practice, *Journal of Geography in Higher Education,* 35:2, 299–309, DOI: 10.1080/03098265.2011.554115

Harris, K. R., Santangelo, T., & Graham, S. (2010). Metacognition and strategies instruction in writing. In H. S. Waters & W. Schneider (Eds.). *Metacognition, strategy use, and instruction*, 226–256. Guilford Press.

Hattie, J. (2015). The applicability of visible learning to higher education. *Scholarship of Teaching and Learning in Psychology*, *1*(1), 79–91. https://doi.org/10.1037/stl0000021

Jensen, A. A. (2015). How does it feel to become a master's student? Boundary crossing and emotions related to understanding a new educational context. In B. Lund and T. Chemi (Eds.). *Dealing with emotions: A pedagogical challenge to innovative learning*, 61–80.

Lakey, G. (2020). *Facilitating group learning strategies: Strategies for success with diverse learners*. PM Press.

Lazarus, R. S. (1999). *Stress and emotion: A new synthesis*. Springer Publishing Co.

Mezirow, J. (2000). Learning to think like an adult: Core concepts of transformation theory. In Mezirow and Associates. *Learning as transformation: Critical perspectives on a theory in progress*, 3–33. Jossey-Bass.

Mintz, S. (2021, January 28). Creating an immersive experience and active participation of students in E-learning during COVID-19. *Higher Education Ethics Watch* [Blog]. https://www.higheredethicswatch.com/

Peck, M. S. (2003). *The road less traveled: A new psychology of love, traditional values and spiritual growth*. Touchstone. Original work published 1978

Pekrun, R., Goetz, T., & Titz, W. (2002). Academic emotions in students' self-regulated learning and achievement: A program of qualitative and quantitative research. *Educational Psychologist*, *37*(2), 91–106.

Próspero, M., Russell, A. C., & Vohra-Gupta, S. (2012, February 8). Effects of motivation and educational attainment: Ethnic and developmental differences among first generation students. *Journal of Hispanic Education 11*(1), 100–119. https://doi.org/10.1177/1538192711435556

Roorda, D. L., Koomen, H. Y., Spilt, J. L., & Oort. F. J. (2011). The influence of effective teacher-student relationships on students' school engagement and achievement: A meta-analytic approach. *Review Educational Research*, *81*(4), 493–529. DOI: 10.310-2/0034654311421793

Silvia, P. (2008). Interest—The curious emotion. *Current Directions in Psychological Science*, *17*(1), 57–60. https://doi.org/10.1111/j.1467-8721.2008.00548.x

Stahl, D. (2021). *Secondary classroom teachers' beliefs and decision making regarding the use of feedback to improve student learning*. [Doctoral honors dissertation, University of St. Thomas]. ProQuest Dissertations and Theses Global.

Steel, P. (2007). The nature of procrastination: A meta-analytic and theoretical review of quintessential self-regulatory failure. *American Psychological Bulletin*, *133*(1), 65–94.

Steel, P., & Klingsieck, K. B. (2016). Academic procrastination: Psychological antecedents revisited. *Australian Psychologist*, *51*(1), 36–46. https://doi.org/10.1111/ap.12173

Waters, H. S., & Kunnmann, T. W. (2010). Metacognition and strategy in early childhood. In H. S. Waters & W. Schneider (Eds.). *Metacognition, strategy use, and instruction*, 3–22. Guilford Press.

Chapter 10

Dear Professor
Inventing New Pedagogies

Sarah Noonan

Dear Teachers and Professors,

I speak for and with my colleagues who wrote this book. We do not claim to know all the answers about teaching and can easily stay up all night telling you stories of our failures. Time is in short supply and the ideas presented here might overwhelm even the most organized and experienced teacher or professor.

My study of expert award-winning professors produced an interesting finding—when professors failed at something and they overcame the problem, they later became experts in the areas they previously failed (Noonan, 2013). Teachers and professors identified the one big thing to change and in doing so, they made improvements in other areas of their practice.

The concepts and strategies presented in this book were drawn from the collective knowledge of disciplinary fields, the scholarship of teaching, and findings from our research studies and experiences about diverse learners. We stayed within our areas of expertise but also collaborated on the ideas together to write this book.

The overarching goal involved describing the needs of diverse learners and then providing specific pedagogies for consideration and experimentation. Culturally responsive pedagogy responds to learner characteristics, offers curriculum tailored to attract students to ensure their success, and "respond[s] to the cultures *actually present* in the classroom" (italics added; Rychly & Graves, 2012, p. 45).

Rychly and Graves (2012) identified four practices needed to adopt and use culturally responsive methods, including "teachers [who] are empathetic and caring, . . . reflective about their [attitudes and] beliefs about people from other cultures . . . [,] reflective about their own cultural frames of reference, and . . . knowledgeable about other cultures" (pp. 45–46). Empathetic and caring teachers are *unwilling to accept low achievement rates* and can see things from students' perspectives (Rychly & Graves, 2012). Students experience caring and empathy from teachers who insist students are capable learners and ensure they experience academic success.

I encourage you to investigate the pedagogies described in each chapter and experiment by adopting one or more methods. When you investigate pedagogy, each chapter offers something different, something new. It might be a combination of factors that resonate with your experiences. You might see something new and say to yourself, "Here it is!" If nothing strikes you as new, perhaps you can experience the satisfaction of confirming your practice.

Underachievement and the achievement gap continue to plague educational systems. All students can learn with clear direction and our support. One thing we can do is serve our students, advocate for change, and figure out how to share pedagogies that produce results.

An audit of practice might include a reflection on the overarching pedagogies for diverse learners and a selection of areas to review for learning and teaching methods. Do your students have opportunities to

- investigate the past and current practice of oppression and its effects, use of privilege and power to maintain the status quo; and the experience of intergenerational trauma?
- engage in radical listening, critical reflection, and dialogue for learning and transformation?
- use critical consciousness and the language of inequality to critique and challenge dominant assumptions and practices?
- experience nurturing relationships, whole-person health, and inclusive learning environments?
- engage in authentic, interdisciplinary, collaborative learning projects and assessments, participate in social learning, and use problem-solving methods?
- experience joyful learning, which benefits students now and later in their lives?
- experience how student identities, learning styles, perspectives, and experiences are recognized and honored?
- identify the root causes of academic disengagement and learn the strategies, habits, and dispositions needed to raise academic performance?
- receive an invitation to learn and experience hope, and benefit from goals, structure, coaching, and "fast" feedback to disrupt a pattern of academic underachievement and procrastination?

- experience empathy and compassion, and know teachers understand student experiences, and trust that their teachers and others are committed to see them through the learning process?

Do you want to join us in exploring pedagogies for diverse learners? I know we would all like to hear about your ideas. Drop me a note and I will share your comments with the all the contributing authors.

Best regards,

Sarah Noonan
sjnoonan@stthomas.edu

PEDAGOGIES FOR DIVERSE LEARNERS SUMMARY

Pedagogies for Diverse Learners: Tools for Discovery and Development offers advice and practical examples on ways to *engage* students in learning. "To" engage refers to the commitment to learning in the role of student, collaborator, and contributor. This includes students' preparation and participation in class, completion of assignments, and demonstrated accomplishment of academic goals. Students demonstrate their accomplishment of academic outcomes based on test results and "artifacts" collected to provide evidence of learning and achievement.

The second meaning of the words "to engage" refers to the teacher's responsibility to plan and facilitate a lesson, unit, or course that attracts and sustains learners' attention and effort. Students engage in learning because they see value in the learning activities and courses. This includes the topic of study, the processes used for learning, the products students create, and the learning environment.

Essentially, the responsibility for ensuring student learning using "pedagogies for diverse learners" requires teachers to achieve a broad understanding of their students and what makes a great course and learning experience. Professors and teachers stand in the middle of a continuum and feel the pull of planning lessons based on learner characteristics and needs on one end and teaching disciplinary knowledge, skills, and dispositions at the other end.

If there is some way to accomplish both ends, good teachers will manage the tension, find a way to attract students to learning, and put them on a steady path to achieving disciplinary knowledge. A caring learning environment with warm and supportive relationships makes all the difference for student and teacher success. The welcome sign should hang on every classroom door. Learning is central to every act of growth.

REFERENCES

Noonan, S. J. (2013). *How real teachers learn to engage all learners*. Rowman & Littlefield.

Rychly, L., & Graves, E. (2012). Teacher characteristics for culturally responsive pedagogy, *Multicultural Perspectives, 14*(1), 44–49.

Index

Page references for figures are italicized.

academic student procrastination (AsP): action research on, 131–32; and appraisal of academic tasks, 138; definition of, 132; hidden costs of, 132–34; seven factors affecting, 135–37; triage assessment of, *130*, 131
ACEs. *See* adverse childhood experiences
adult learners: motivation of, 61; and self-directed learning, 61
adverse childhood experiences (ACEs): and curricular modifications, 53–54; definition of, 53; prevalence of, 53
affective pedagogies: relationship development, 78–79; student expertise, 76–78, 81; teacher engagement and energy, 81–82; teacher movement, 83–84; teaching valued above content, 79–81
ambiguous loss: definition of, 40; effects and the future, 40
anti-oppressive practice: arts, observation, and experience of, 45; definition of, viii; and four-step process, 45; and interrupting cycles of systemic oppression, 17

AsP. *See* academic student procrastination

Bandura, A., 50, 145, 159–60
BIPOC. *See* Black, Indigenous, and people of color
Black, Indigenous, and people of color (BIPOC), 110
Black Lives Matter, response to Trayvon Martin's death, 38
Brooks, G., 45–46

Carello, J., 56–57
Castile, Philando: death of, 28–29; death live-streamed by Diamond Phillips, 29; public outrage and community meetings after, 29; and sharing a meal, 29
Center for Law and Social Policy (CLASP), 49
centering identity: and analyzing experience, 119; and audit of teaching philosophy, 126; and critical thinking and, 120–22; definition of, 110; in education, 112; and identity salience, 113; pedagogical approaches to, 119; and recognizing

systemic oppression, 110; and social identities, 114; and tools to reflect on experience, 126

CLASP. *See* Center for Law and Social Policy

cognitive bias and decision-making, 26; and effects of split-second decisions, 26; and stereotypic associations, 27; and unconscious bias, 27

collaboration: courageous conversations and, 123; and engagement in learning, 139; and novelty, 63, 81, 125, 139; and social change, 22; and trauma-informed care, 56, 122

coming to grips with loss: definition of, 39; goals of, 39; stages of, 39–40; triggers in, 40; turning points in, 40

corequisite remediation, 152

COVID–19: and decline in student performance, 129–31; excessive stress and, 50; as a factor affecting academic success, 50; and gap in education and learning loss, 142–43; and health disparities, 54; and incivility, 65; and isolation, 51, 65; and lack of private spaces for online learning, 51; and lack of technical skills, 61; and the pivot, 6, 142

critical events: call for change as, 42; definition of, 41; and quest narrative, 41; and systemic racism, 38–39, 42

critical reflection: definition of, 30; and gaining new perspectives, three stages of, 30

cultural humility: and discovery process, 114; positionality and, 114

curriculum: and acting for social change, 46–47; and critical consciousness and Black students, 46; culturally relevant, 2, 13–15; culturally responsive, 13–14, 60, 118, 173; culturally sustaining, 92–93, 106, 116, 118–19, 122; and interrogating racism, 46; and the language of inequality, 46; and learning styles, ix, 81, 174; modifications, viii; and scaffolding, 89; and student choice, 15–16, 53, 161

dark tourism, 42
DAW. *See* digital audio workstation
development phase, vii
dialogue, definition of, 22, 33
digital audio workstation (DAW), 90
discovery phase, vii

Ellis, K., 74–75
emotional intelligence, 71, 77
emotions: achievement, 161; epistemic, 161–62; negative, 143; social, 162; topic, 162
engaging in learning: and academic success, 138–40; definition of, 176; and exemplary teachers and six tenets, 76–84; and interdisciplinary ways of learning and teaching, 88, 174; and interesting and worthy content, 139; and student self-appraisal, 138–39

Floyd, George: death of, 42–43; and George Floyd Square, 42
Freire, P., 22, 30, 33, 38
French, B. H., 58

Hamilton: An American Musical, and Caribbean migration and hip-hop, 87
historical empathy: and covering the content, 25; and the culprit's actions, 25; definition of, 25; inquiry methods and case studies of, 25
historically privileged groups, 111

identity: exclusion of, 112; and honoring, 115; and learning-centered outcomes, 116; and philosophy of teaching, 115; and salience in education, 111–13; and social identity groups, 111

IGD. *See* intergroup dialogue
Indigenous children: and boarding schools, 4–8, 112; deculturalization of, 111
intensive assistance and recovery pedagogies: and coaching, 165–66; and "fast" feedback, 166; and an invitation to learn and hope, 163–64; and nurturing relationships, 163; and prevention and intervention strategies, 166; and structure and self-regulation, 164
interdisciplinary curriculum, 88; and My American Story, 87–108
interest, tasks and types of, 155–56
intergenerational trauma: boarding schools and, 4–8, 26, 112; root causes of, 36; and wounds, 38, 174
intergroup dialogue (IGD): definition of, 122; phases of, 122–25

Klingsieck, J. B., 133
Kishimoto, K., 59
knowledge, skills, and dispositions (KSD): definition of, 140–41; and doing "professional" work, 141; and strategy discovery, 154–55; and strategy instruction, 153–54; and types of knowledge, 153
Krathwohl, D., 71
KSD. *See* knowledge, skills, and dispositions

Ladson-Billings, G., 14
learning loss: definition of, 143; effects on student learning, 143; negative academic emotions, 143
lesbian, gay, bisexual, transgender, queer or questioning, intersex, asexual and more (LGBTQIA+), 119–20
LGBTQIA+. *See* lesbian, gay, bisexual, transgender, queer or questioning, intersex, asexual and more

major life event: definition of, 145; interrupting academic program, 145; and providing academic and emotional support, 145
Martin, Trayvon: and the Conversation, 39; death of, 37; and lesson design, 43–45; parent and community response to death of, 37; and Sunday sermons, 38
Mezirow, J., 159, 169
mindfulness: and critical self-reflection, 125; and difficult conservations, 125–26; and emphasis on systemic inequities, oppression, and power, 125
Miranda, L., 87
musicking: definition of, 89; and songwriting and digital music production, 89
My American Story: composing a song in, 97, 100–102; creative notes in, 96; end-of-unit creative projects in, 97–98; examples of, 100–105; and identity, 106; and listening journals, 97; modules, 91–92; presentation and critique of, 102–9; structure of, 98; summative assessments of, 88–90; using critical and creative thinking skills and, 93–94; writing an artist statement in, 102

National Sleep Foundation (NSF), 64
Native American history: absent narrative, 1; boarding schools, 5–8; genocide, 2; historical trauma, 3; Tribal nations, 3; Whitewashing history, 9, 11–12
Native pedagogies: culturally responsive curriculum, 13, 14; definition of, 13; gaining an awareness of oppression, 30–31; Indigenous knowledge systems, 14–15; interdisciplinary curriculum, 16; projects and location-based pedagogy, 16; relationships,

13; traditional ways of teaching, 15–16; and values, 15
Native students: and code-switching, 11; and cultural norms, 10; and cultural obligations and taxation, 10; identity, 9; learning experiences in predominately White institutions (PWIs) of, 12; and living in two worlds, 2–5, 17; and need for personal connection, 2, 11–12; and racism and implicit bias, 2, 5, 8–10
nontraditional learners: description of, 49; and reasons to enroll in college, 49; and reasons to leave college, 49–50
NSF. *See* National Sleep Foundation

online learning: advantages of, 61; building trust and relationships in, 84; collaboration and co-learning in, 61, 84; effective teaching strategies for, 62; facilitating adult learning in, 62; feedback in, 166; and lack of technical skills, 61, 131; learning loss in, 134; teacher movement in, 83; tensions between relationships and the content in, 63, 79–81

pedagogies for diverse learners, ten key "meta" strategies, viii–ix
PRH. *See* psychology of race-based healing
psychology of race-based healing (PRH), and five core anchors, 58

race-based traumatic stress (RBTS): definition of, 54; and internalized racism, 54; and psychological distress, 54; and race-based healing, 58
racism: definition of, 26; and racially motivated incidents, 109; roots of, 26
radical listening: definition of, 21; giving voice, 22; and teacher talk, 77

radical love, 33
RBTS. *See* race-based traumatic stress
relational turning points: definition of, 73; four distinct categories, 73–74
Rice, Tamir: death of, 28; and police assumptions and threat analysis, 28; and protests and community meals, 29

SAMHSA. *See* The Substance Abuse and Mental Health Service Association
secret sauce and exemplary teachers, 85
self-efficacy: and conscientiousness and decline in self-regulation, 150; definition of, 145: and the experience of stress and coping, 145–46; and facet scales, 150
sleep deprivation: as associated with racial and ethnic discrimination, 64; effects on cognitive performance of, 64; and stress, 63
Small, C., 89
social justice: and healing pedagogies, *23*; and critical events, leadership, the call to action and change, 33; and goals, 47; and history, culture, language, and traditions, 24–25; and raising critical consciousness, 30 –31; and the roots of systemic racism and discrimination, 26–30; six primary strategies in, 22–23; storytelling and the arts in, 33–35; and wounds, culprits, and transformation, 33–37
spirituality: and the search for purpose and meaning, 59; values of, 60
spiritual responsive pedagogy, 59; and anti-racist pedagogy, 69; definition of, 59–60; and ethical and moral life, 60; and social justice leadership, viii, 33, 41
Stell, P., 133
stories: definition of, 35; four types of, 35

storytelling: and community building, 88; and democracy, 107; and identity formation, 88; and social activism, 88

strategies to bolster student success, *151*

stress: and adult learners, 50; and burnout, 50–51; and overload, roles, and responsibilities, 144

The Substance Abuse and Mental Health Service Association (SAMHSA), 52

suspicion heuristic: definition of, 27; and unconscious bias and programming, 27

Taylor, Breonna: call for change, 4; death of, 40–41; and no-knock warrants, 41; and police accountability and brutality, 41, 46

teacher confirmation: affective and support dimensions of, 73; at-risk students, 73; and behaviors, 75 decline in the secondary level, 7; definition of, 74; impact on student engagement in learning, 72; teacher-student relationships (TSRs), self-efficacy, and, 74–75; and trust, 72

TIC. *See* trauma-informed care

transformation: definition of, 41; and identity change, 169; and intense listening and dialogue, 60

trauma: definition of, 52; effects on student learning, 53; interventions, 55; prevalence of, 52

trauma-informed care (TIC): definition of, 55; and self-disclosure, 58–59

Turino, T., 89–90, 94–96

UDL. *See* Universal Design for Learning

unconscious bias: and cultural humility, 115; definition of, 114

Universal Design for Learning (UDL), 116; curating course materials in, 117; and fostering creativity in activities and assessments, 118

wellness hub, 64–65

About the Contributors

Derrick Crim, EdD, LADC, CPPR, associate professor, Metropolitan State University; spiritual care professional, Hazelden Betty Ford Foundation. Crim received a master's in addiction studies from the Hazelden Graduate School of Addiction Studies, a doctor of education in leadership from the University of St. Thomas, and a master's in pastoral ministry from the St. Paul Seminary and School of Divinity. Contact via (24) Dr. Derrick E. Crim, EdD, LADC, CPPR, MAPM | LinkedIn.

Penelope Dupris, EdD, serves as an assistant principal at Brooklyn Center Community Schools, Minneapolis, Minnesota. As a Native woman and educator, academic success for students of color has been Dupris's main priority. Dupris advocates for social justice and improvement in education for Indigenous students. Dupris's research focuses on Native students and pedagogy, social justice, and intergenerational trauma and its effects on Native communities. Contact via pfdupris@gmail.com.

Christina Holmgren is a Black, cisgender woman, scholar, and educator with over a decade of experience working within higher education. Her leadership experience includes the recruitment and retention of diverse student populations, with a focus on accessibility, inclusivity, and equity. Her scholarship and research interests include racial identity development, trauma-informed pedagogical practice, Black feminist thought, and culturally sustaining pedagogy. You can learn more about her work and research via LinkedIn at https://www.linkedin.com/in/christinajholmgren-she-her-4b9662188.

Sarah J. Noonan, EdD, is an executive fellow and professor emerita at the University of St. Thomas. Professional experience includes serving as a K–12 teacher, administrator, and superintendent of schools as well as department chair and member of higher education faculty. Noonan's research focuses on the scholarship of learning and teaching, academic student procrastination, educational leadership, and doctoral education and academic writing (chaired 52 dissertations). Contact via sjnoonan@stthomas.edu.

Ilah Raleigh, EdD, is the director of visual and performing arts at the Blake School in Hopkins, Minnesota. She began her dual careers as an arts educator and performing artist teaching piano to youth in her Minneapolis neighborhood, followed by two years studying voice with Giulietta Simionato in Milan, Italy. Ilah Raleigh's performance career has led her to the stages of the Washington National Opera, Wolf Trap Opera, and Minnesota Opera, while serving varied roles in community education, PK–12 education, and higher education. Her website is www.ilahraleigh.com.

Jayne Sommers, PhD (she/her), is a White, cisgender woman, educator, and scholar. Jayne has a decade of experience working in undergraduate student-facing positions in various higher education institutions. Currently an associate professor and chair of the Department of Educational Leadership at the University of St. Thomas, her teaching and scholarly interests coalesce around transforming education to serve, honor, and center the lived experiences of historically excluded populations. Contact via jayneksommers@stthomas.edu.

Gail L. Weinhold, EdD, has worked for more than 25 years in education, first as a secondary English teacher and for more than a decade in teacher education. She is a full professor and director of faculty development at North Central University in Minneapolis, Minnesota. Her research interests include student engagement, teacher self-efficacy, and affective and performance-enhanced teaching. Contact via https://www.linkedin.com/in/gailweinhold.

Aura Wharton-Beck, EdD, currently serves as an assistant professor in the Department of Educational Leadership and a Diversity, Equity, and Inclusion (DEI) Fellow at the University of St. Thomas. Wharton-Beck's professional career includes serving as an elementary and middle school teacher, a school district mentor teacher, an elementary school principal, and an adjunct faculty member in higher education. Wharton-Beck's research agenda focuses on diverse feminist perspectives, school leadership, social justice and healing pedagogies, African American women's history, and the intersectionality of public policy, race, class, transportation, and housing. Contact via anwhartobec@stthomas.edu.

www.ingramcontent.com/pod-product-compliance
Lightning Source LLC
Chambersburg PA
CBHW032025230426
43671CB00005B/204